D1740802

RABBI YAAKOV WEINBERG

FUNDAMENTALS and FAITH

INSIGHTS INTO THE RAMBAM'S 13 PRINCIPLES

Edited by
Rabbi Mordechai Blumenfeld

TARGUM / FELDHEIM

First published 1991

Phototypeset at Targum Press

Published by:
Targum Press Inc.
22700 W. Eleven Mile Rd.
Southfield, Mich. 48034

in conjunction with:
Mishnas Rishonim

Distributed by:
Feldheim Publishers
200 Airport Executive Park
Spring Valley, N.Y. 10977

Distributed in Israel by:
Nof Books Ltd.
POB 23646
Jerusalem 91235

Printed in Israel

ישיבת נר ישראל

NER ISRAEL RABBINICAL COLLEGE
400 MT. WILSON LANE
BALTIMORE, MARYLAND 21208

In a few short paragraphs the Rambam set down, clearly and in order, the basic awarenesses of the Jewish credo. In doing so he created a highway to understanding the fundamental requirements of relating to and serving the Creator and Maintainer of the Universe.

It is impossible to exaggerate the importance of an exposition of the meaning and significance of the Rambam's presentation. I have tried to convey some of the depths and implications of these statements in a series of *shiurim*.

I am deeply grateful to Rav Mordechai Blumenfeld, who has graciously undertaken to put in writing the essence of these *shiurim*. It is a difficult undertaking, indeed, to present in the concise form required in writing a book the deep and subtle thoughts of the Rambam. I believe that Rav Blumenfeld has been successful in doing so.

It is apparent to me that this has been a labor of love and for this, too, I am very grateful.

Yaakov Weinberg

In Appreciation

My wife's loving parents,
Rabbi Avraham and Rochel Berger,
whose foresight and generosity has made this work possible.
May they only know *nachas* and joy from their
children and grandchildren.

Ernest Wuliger,
a giant of industry, whose unwavering support
has been a source of inspiration.

In memory of

Mordechai ben Moshe *z"l*

by his daughters
Sarita, Hedy, Loretta Roesnhaus
Miami, Florida

Special thanks to:

Dov and Nancy Friedberg
Toronto, Canada

Herb and Joyce Green
Toronto, Canada

The Diena family, children, and grandchildren
Toronto, Canada

in memory of
Rav David and Ida Diena

Many thanks to:

Dennis and Robin Berman
Baltimore, Maryland

Nathan and Shani Bleeman
Toronto, Canada

Mordechai and Esther Hackerman
Baltimore, Maryland

Yehoshua and Leah Honingwachs
New York, New York

Mendy and Marilyn Maierovitz
Toronto, Canada

David and Cyna Singer ·
New York, New York

H. Wayne Tannenbaum
Toronto, Canada

Aharon and Susie Bleeman
Toronto, Canada

Don and Marion Meyers
New York, New York

in memory of

Harry D. Greenman
London, England

Acknowledgments

Mrs. Melanie Zeldman
for her patience and energy in
proofreading the original manuscript.

Mr. Shalom Dovid Kaplan
for editing and proofreading the final manuscript.

Contents

Introduction

The Uniqueness of the Principles

The Rambam's Thirteen Principles of Faith are only a minuscule representation of the literally thousands upon thousands of tenets of Judaism. Why did the Rambam select these particular Principles? What criteria determined his choice?

Perhaps these Principles are significant because they cannot be rejected by one who desires to adhere to Judaism. A denial of these Principles certainly results in an estrangement from Judaism and Torah.[1] However, there are many other tenets whose rejection also brings about this estrangement. The Rambam himself states that rejecting any word of

---

1. The Rambam in his *Commentary to the Mishnah* (*Sanhedrin* 10:1), after presenting the Thirteen Principles, comments that the individual who does not believe each of these Principles leaves the community of Israel, denies the essence of the Almighty, and is called a sectarian and an *apikorus* (apostate).

the Torah brings about such an estrangement.[2] It would seem that these Principles are not unique in these terms; in this vein, the Thirteen Principles are but a few of many others.

Rather, these Principles are unique as those tenets which one must be aware of and accept in order to be considered a practicing Jew. According to the Rambam, their acceptance defines the minimum requirement necessary for one to relate to the Almighty and His Torah as a member of the People of Israel.

The Unfortunate Apikorus

The words of Rav Chaim of Brisk provide further insight into the significance of these Principles. He has spoken of an individual who is, "unfortunately, an *apikorus*."[3] The Yiddish phrase, "*nebach*, an *apikorus*," reflects a deep feeling of pity for the poor person who, perhaps through no fault of his own, became estranged from Judaism. To whom was Rav Chaim referring?

In his *Mishneh Torah* (Laws of Repentance 3:6-8), Rambam includes *apikorsim* among those who do not have a share in the World to Come. *Apikorsim* are: those who deny prophecy, asserting that there is no communication between God and man; those who accept prophecy but deny the specific prophecy of Moshe Rabbeinu; and those who believe that the Creator does not know the actions of man.

2. Ibid. For example, if one attributes even one word of the Torah to Moshe rather than God, he denies the entire Torah and has no share in the World to Come.

3. A term denoting anyone who belittles and despises Torah and its students. The Rambam in his *Commentary to the Mishnah*, after defining this word, comments that he who denies the fundamental Principles of Torah is also considered an *apikorus*. See notes 1 and 2.

The term *apikorus* usually connotes an educated person who knows what he should do but refuses to do it. In asserting his independence, he throws off the yoke of responsibility to adhere to Jewish law. Although he may reject only one mitzvah, it affects his entire status as an observant Jew. There would be no sigh of pity from Rav Chaim for this man, for he has *chosen* to estrange himself from Judaism.

On the other hand, Rav Chaim was not referring to someone ignorant of mitzvos. He is categorized by the Sages as a "captured child".[4] This category includes anyone not raised and educated in the ways of the Torah. The "captured child", deprived of a Jewish education, is exempt from most of the consequences of not fulfilling his responsibilities. Unfortunately, in our present day and age, what was once only the result of a violent tragedy—a Jewish child taken into captivity and raised by gentiles—has become the lot and status of the majority of our People. Clearly, ignorance of a specific mitzvah does not make one an *apikorus*.

Actually, Rav Chaim's sympathy was directed towards

---

4. In his *Mishneh Torah* (Laws of Rebels 3:3), Rambam writes:

> This applies only to one who repudiates the Oral Law in his thought and conclusions, and who goes according to his easy conclusions in the stubbornness of his heart, denying first the Oral Law, as did Zadok and Boethus and all who went astray. But [regarding] their children and grandchildren—who were misguided by their parents and born among the Karaites, who trained them in their views—[each] is like a child taken captive by them and raised by them, [such that] he is not quick to grasp the ways of the mitzvos. For he is like an *anoos* [one who abjures Judaism under duress] and even though he later learns that he is a Jew—and observes Jews and their religion—he is regarded as an *anoos*, since he was reared in error. Thus it is with those we mentioned, who adhere to the practices of their Karaite parents who went astray. Therefore, efforts should be made to bring them back in repentance, to draw them near by friendly relations, until they return to the strength-giving source, the Torah.

an individual who possesses certain erroneous beliefs or lacks certain necessary beliefs concerning God and His Torah. In turn, these shortcomings create an inaccurate and invalid *approach* to the mitzvos, which ultimately results in this individual's inability to be an accurately practicing Jew. This is the "unfortunate *apikorus*" to whom Rav Chaim referred. He may be considered an *apikorus*, because in reality—although possibly not in practice—he is estranged from the Torah.

The Thirteen Principles of the Rambam represent precisely that area of "faith orientation" with which Rav Chaim is concerned. These tenets of Judaism are absolutely necessary to properly relate to Torah. Without them, an individual is estranged from Torah; he is an "unfortunate *apikorus*."

Accepting God's Sovereignty

An illustration is given[5] of a new king who came to a country. The people there told him, "Decree laws for us." He replied: "When you will accept my sovereignty, I will decree laws for you; if you will not accept my sovereignty, you will also not accept my laws." Similarly, the Almighty said to the People of Israel, "I am God, your Lord, who took you out of the land of Egypt, the house of slavery. You shall have no other gods." This implies that God first asked the question, "Am I the Sovereign you have accepted?" Only when the Jews had accepted God as their King could the Almighty then give them their laws.

The Mishnah states, "All of Israel have a share in the World to Come."[6] Every Jew, because he is part of the Chosen Nation which made its Covenant with God, has a share in the World to Come. According to the Rambam's understanding of the mishnah, however, a Jew is considered part of

---

5. *Mechilta, parashas Yisro.*

6. *Sanhedrin,* ch. 10.

Israel only when he accepts the Sovereignty of the Almighty. Before he can relate to the mitzvos of the Torah, before he can share in the destiny of the Jewish People, he must first accept God's Kingship.

But how does one accept the Sovereignty of God? What is the meaning and implication of "I am God, your Lord, who took you out of the land of Egypt, the house of slavery"? It is in his commentary to this very mishnah that the Rambam presents his Thirteen Principles of Faith. It is through these Principles, he says, that one learns to accept the Sovereignty of the Almighty.

Ethics of Convenience

A Jew has free will: he may choose to adhere to the Torah or to reject it. The most basic premise of the Principles communicates that a god which does not bind the individual, but rather allows him freedom to do as he desires, is not God. What's more, a law that does not bind the individual, which allows him freedom to do as he pleases, is not the Torah. If one is able to select, change, and arbitrate the Commandments, then the very nature of the Torah and the relationship one has to its Giver is radically altered. One deviation from the behavior dictated by the Torah would not destroy it, but the decision itself to make changes, to decide what to do and what not to do, necessarily indicates the perversion of Torah. If the nature of God was such that man could avoid His wrath, if the nature of God's communication to man was such that it could be altered, then man would be able to choose acceptance of Torah while not being bound by it. But if one perceives that he can escape the notice of God, he has no God.

To appreciate that man cannot avoid the wrath of the Almighty, or change the Instructions for Life that He has given Israel, is to appreciate the Sovereignty of God. The individual who feels he is not bound by the Torah, who believes he can escape God's notice, cannot truly relate to Him as a sovereign.

The Thirteen Principles render the Torah absolutely binding. They leave no loophole, no freedom for man to twist and pervert the commandments. Their message is clear: God is and must be the sole arbiter of what is right and what is wrong, what is good and what is bad—absolutely God, and not man.

For if man is the arbiter, then there exists no good or bad, no right or wrong, only a situation of convenience. And if there is one thing to which the history of mankind testifies with deepest eloquence and without any ambiguity, it is that dependence upon man's sensibilities is a totally ineffective guide for human action. To give man free rein on his actions, depending only upon his own prudence, inevitably leads to man doing what is most convenient, disregarding any attempt to realize absolute right or wrong. If one is not bound by these Thirteen Principles, then it is man's subjectivity, not God's wisdom, that becomes the decisive factor in his choice of actions.

For example, it is historically evident that religious law which allows for continuously self-revising prophecy will be updated with whatever revelation is necessary to allow man the utmost convenience and comfort. The Mormon Church functions as a good illustration. At the outset, the Church did not allow blacks to enter into its fold. When it became too uncomfortable to defend this racist policy, however, the necessary "revelation" occurred in order to conveniently change it. In contrast, Rambam's seventh Principle, differentiating between Torah prophecy and the prophecy that followed the death of Moshe Rabbeinu, asserts that prophecy with the power to revise original law is not possible.

With the Thirteen Principles, the Rambam teaches that it is not enough to know that there is a Creator. One must also be aware of several specific realities of the Creator. Reflecting on these specific realities—God's absolute, eternal, and incorporeal Being—requires a sophisticated intellectual awareness. The person whose faith does not include such an awareness of the Creator has no way of relating to Judaism. The more subtle corollary involves the person whose faith in God allows him to believe that He actually has a hand or a temper. It is not so clear why such an erroneous belief also estranges him from Judaism. It is the goal of this book to discover why such details are so essential in making the difference between being estranged from all or part of Judaism.

The Components of a Religion

It is generally accepted that in order for a particular belief system to be called a religion, it must have at least three components:

1) Recognition of a Divine Being that is to be worshipped.

2) Instructions as to how He is to be worshipped.

3) Reward and punishment for carrying out or failing to carry out His instructions.

A system of social norms may exist without these, but not a religion.

The Rambam's Thirteen Principles are an elaboration of these three points as they are realized in Judaism. Of the thirteen, there are five principles concerning the reality of the Creator, four concerning His Torah, and four concerning reward and punishment. Since these general concepts of the existence of the Creator, of instructions from the Creator, and of reward and punishment are common to all religions, it is the details of these concepts that establish the uniqueness of Judaism.

Reward and Punishment

It is obvious that without a God and without God's communication to man, there can be no Torah. It is not as obvious that without the awareness of reward and punishment, Torah cannot exist. This third component, developed in the four Principles concerning reward and punishment, demands an explanation. Aren't we admonished not to serve God out of either fear of punishment or aspiration for reward? Doesn't the Mishnah[7] quote Antigonus of Socho: "Be not like the servants who serve the master on the condition of receiving reward. Rather, be like the servants who serve the master without the condition of receiving reward"? We know that there is a God and we know that He gave the Torah desiring we keep it. Given these precepts, why must there be an awareness of reward and punishment?

As previously mentioned, the basic premise that is implied in these Principles is that belief in a god or in a religious law that does not bind the individual, but instead allows him freedom to do as he desires, inhibits the possibility of relating to God and Torah. He who is willing to keep the laws of the Torah because of cultural reasons, or because he feels that the Torah is a wonderful discipline which motivates him to a healthy and productive life, is not observing Judaism.

Parallel to this idea, one who feels he can choose to observe the commandments, without being aware of the consequences of his choices, may estrange himself from Judaism. Without reward and punishment, without consequences, it is an individual's choice to fulfill the commandments or not to fulfill the commandments. He is not bound in any way. When the choice is left up to the individual to observe the Torah laws and the going gets rough, it becomes easy to rationalize some time off. That little time off will grow and

---

7. *Pirkei Avos* 1:3.

before long he will end up with no observance of the laws. An awareness of consequences, reward and punishment, makes the difference between having a real Torah and not having a real Torah in our lives.

However, the issue of consequences regarding the fulfillment of mitzvos is really much deeper than this. Without reward and punishment, without reaction from God, there is no One to serve. To relate to a perceived Creator who shows no interest in man's actions is impossible. Seen in human terms, one cannot love without his loved one being aware of and reacting to his efforts. Can one give a gift if it doesn't make a difference to the recipient whether he has received it? When an individual meets with indifference to his efforts, he feels rejected. If a parent does not react to a child by showing approval or disapproval, the child feels completely rejected. Even if the parent verbally proclaims his love for the child, if he doesn't react to his behavior, the child will know he is a liar. There is no in-between: either a parent rewards or punishes his child or he is indifferent to him. Even a parent's cruelest reaction can be less traumatic than no reaction at all.

In truth, God is not indifferent to His creation: He does not reject us. On the contrary, He reacts through reward and punishment, demonstrating His concern. A favorable reaction from the Almighty to man's endeavors is perceived as a reward; an unfavorable reaction is perceived as a punishment. In the same manner, a person's smile is perceived as a reward, and his frown as a punishment.

A world without reward and punishment is a world of utter indifference, and indifference is the ultimate rejection. One cannot serve indifference. In order for there to be a relationship between God and man, God must react to man's actions. Our awareness of this reaction, reward or punishment, informs us that the Almighty cares, that our actions make a difference. Without reward and punishment life has no meaning—for what man would or would not do would make no difference.

The last four Principles of the Rambam, dealing with reward and punishment, affirm that a person's actions make a difference. They teach us to evaluate our personal triumphs and frustrations in light of the Almighty's response to our behavior. On a global scale, they teach us to view world events in this same light and not to interpret them in terms of natural, political, or sociological cause and effect.

Those Who Disagreed

It should be stressed that all Torah scholars agree on the validity and significance of the Principles. However, some of the Rambam's contemporaries questioned whether a lack of awareness of or belief in several of the Principles would result in an actual estrangement from Judaism.

The Raavad,[8] for example, says that although it is foolish and incorrect to take the Torah's reference to the "hand of God" literally, those who believe God to be corporeal can still relate to Torah as members of the Jewish community.

Other Rishonim maintain that the Jew raised among the gentiles can still fulfill mitzvos, even if he is not aware of God's promise concerning the coming of the Mashiach. Granted, the educated and learned Jew who denies that history will culminate in the coming of the Mashiach is an *apikorus* and has estranged himself from Judaism, but the ignorant individual, they say, whose beliefs do not include the Mashiach, can still keep Shabbos and observe the laws of *kashrus*; he can live in a sukkah and eat matzah on Pesach. Despite his ignorance, he remains part of the Jewish community.

---

8. See Rambam, *Mishneh Torah*, Laws of Repentance 3:7.

The Rambam disagrees. He states that without the understanding and awareness of the Mashiach, the Shabbos
that an individual keeps or the laws of *kashrus* he fulfills are
performed as an estranged Jew who is not part of the community of Israel. Such an individual's approach to the mitzvos and his understanding of the nature of his commitment
lack a basic element.

In general, all of the various disputes regarding the Thirteen Principles are of this nature, concerned not with the
validity of the Principles but with the consequences of not
knowing or believing them.

Ikarim Defined

Rav Yosef Albo, in his well-known *Sefer HaIkarim*, challenges the paradigm of the Rambam's Thirteen Principles.
This challenge is quoted almost verbatim by Rav Yitzchak
Abravanel in *Rosh Amanah*, written in defense of the Rambam. Some of Rav Albo's objections relate to the significance of the word *ikar*, one of the Hebrew terms used by the
Rambam and commonly translated as "principle". He likens
the word to the *ikarim*, roots, of a tree. By this definition, the
Thirteen *Ikarim* would be the foundations of Judaism. Just as
the roots of a tree are necessary for its existence, belief in
these principles, these "roots", is necessary to be considered
a practicing Jew.

Assuming this definition, Rav Albo challenges five of
the thirteen Principles. Would an individual's relationship to
the whole Torah be affected if he would not believe in them
or be unaware of them? He asserts that the second Principle,
concerning the unity of the Almighty, and the third Principle, concerning God's incorporeality, do not meet this crite-
rion: "If one were to believe differently, the entire Torah would
not be destroyed nor would his mitzvos be nullified." Simi-

larly, he also asks: "If one would believe that God is truth and His Torah truth but would pray through an intermediary [the fifth Principle], why would this affect his relationship to the entire Torah?" In the same manner, the Rambam's twelfth and thirteenth Principles, involving belief in the coming of the Mashiach and the resurrection of the dead, are not seen as foundations that support one's entire relationship with Torah.

An alternative to this approach is to assume that the Rambam is not listing principles that are absolutely fundamental; rather, they are true and important. Abravanel, in his first proposition in defense of the Rambam, suggests this possibility. He demonstrates that though the words *shoresh* (root) and *yesod* (foundation) are used to signify an absolutely necessary base that supports an entire structure, the word *ikar* can be used as well to signify an important idea or principle. In this connotation *ikar* does not necessarily imply that which serves as a root.

To support this proposal, Abravanel cites the Rambam in his *Commentary to the Mishnah*, in which he states, "The *ikarim* of our religion and its *yesodos* are thirteen." Abravanel asserts that the Rambam's use of both terms there is intentional, in order to include those tenets upon which the entire Torah is dependent (foundations-*yesodos*) as well as those tenets which are important beliefs (principles-*ikarim*). According to the Abravanel, these beliefs, although significant, are not in the same category as the foundations.

This alternative encounters various obstacles. Rav Albo suggests many other "true and praiseworthy beliefs" that could have been included. Why didn't the Rambam include the belief that the *Shechinah* dwells in Israel, or belief in Creation, or belief in the miracles of the Torah, he asks. Furthermore, the Rambam himself clearly states that he who believes in all of the Principles is to be considered part of the People of Israel and has a share in the World to Come, whereas rejecting any of the Principles estranges one from Israel. The Rambam emphasizes "these Principles", not others. Clearly, according to the Rambam, these Principles are axiomatic. They are the foundations of the Jew's relationship to his People, to Torah, and to his Creator.

Clarifying the significance and uniqueness of each of the Thirteen Principles provided the theme for a series of lectures given by Rav Yaakov Weinberg, *shlita*, Rosh Yeshiva of Ner Israel Yeshiva of Baltimore, Maryland. These lectures were given in Ner Israel, and in Yeshivas Aish HaTorah in Yerushalayim. Through the Rosh Yeshiva's insights, the answer to those who challenged the Rambam becomes clear. This answer not only clarifies the paradigm of the Thirteen Principles, it offers an understanding of the ultimate significance of having a God who cares about man and his actions.

Part I
The Existence of God

The First Principle

God as Creator

To believe in the existence of the Creator, may He be blessed, i.e., that there is an Existence that is perfect [and absolute] in all facets of existence. He is the cause of all that exists, the sustenance of all, and through Him all is maintained. There is no possibility that He does not exist because without Him, all existence would cease to be and nothing would remain. [Whereas] if we would imagine the absence of all existence other than His, the existence of God would neither cease nor diminish. For He is self-sufficient in His existence, He suffices in Himself, and His existence requires nothing other than Himself. [For] among the intelligences—the angels and the constellations and all that they contain and all that is below them—they all need Him for their existence. This is the first Principle, as affirmed by the verse (Exodus 20:2) "I am God, your Lord...."

The First Principle

God as Creator

He is Absolute

The first Principle is to be aware and to know that there is a Primal Cause, a Being whose existence is absolute and from whose existence all existence stems. He alone and only He is absolute. He exists because He exists. It is inconceivable that He not be. His existence has no cause. There is nothing that supports Him. There is nothing that maintains Him. There is no agency through which He came into being. In contrast, everything else that exists is dependent and contingent upon His existence. Nothing else exists in and of itself and independent of Him. Everything else exists only because He wills its existence. He gives everything else its existence and He maintains it.

The question we must now address is why this seemingly abstruse and abstract philosophical point, an affirmation of God's absolute existence and creation's absolute contingency, should determine one's ability to fulfill Torah. What of the simple Jew? Lacking the sophistication to understand both this absolute and this absolute dependency, this Jew approaches the whole issue in the following manner. He knows that there exists a Creator and a creation. He knows that this Creator made the world and watches over it. Perhaps he even has a vague understanding of the difference between a Creator and a creation, but he fails to appreciate that only the Creator is absolute existence, that all other existence is dependent upon Him. What difference does this shortcoming in his understanding of reality make?

His Truth is Absolute

The reason why an appreciation of God's absolute existence and of creation's absolute contingency is so important is that only through His absolute existence can there exist an absolute truth. If the Creator were not absolute but dependent upon something else, He could not claim absolute Truth. Instead, only truth based upon the Creator's source could exist as absolute.

The Torah's truth depends upon its being a derivative of the Absolute Being. If one is not aware of the Almighty's absoluteness, then a Torah with absolute values cannot exist for him, cannot bind him. Instead, a Torah with concepts relative to one's situation would exist. Concepts of good and evil can only be absolute when derived from an absolute source. If derived from a contingent source, they will be seen relative to the situation through the individual's immediate, subjective perception.

The Dangers of Relative Ethics

Relative ethics are meaningless. They create an opportunity in which one does what he feels like doing and then creates the justification for it. If one wants to kill the elderly, he may use the justification that the quality of life is more important than life itself. Thus, murder becomes an act of loving-kindness, in which the murderer is viewed as a sensitive individual who wants to relieve a poor sufferer of a life without quality. If it is a fetus one wants to kill, he may first rationalize that it isn't yet alive. Then he need only pay tribute to the dignity of the living in order to rationalize the acceptability and justice of abortion.

In today's society, those who are concerned with being ethical are forced to embrace humanism and relative ethics. They begin searching for the words to justify what they would like to do. The process is not that difficult; the right words or expression can always be found. In retrospect, perhaps the world needed a Hitler to demonstrate that there is no action which a human being cannot justify, to himself and even to others.

The possibility of absolute good and evil depends upon the existence of an absolute truth. But truth can be absolute only if the Creator is an Absolute Being, since that which He creates and that which is derived from Him can only then reflect the absolute truth of His Being. All of Torah, all morality, and all ethics are contingent upon this principle of God's absoluteness.

Achieving True Existence

Because our existence is contingent upon God, we arrive at the ultimate reality of life only through becoming connected to Him.

Psychologists have many different ideas concerning man's basic drives. Freud's libido, the drive for sensual pleasure, is one proposition, Adler's striving for superiority is another. Napoleon needed to know that after he died there would be statues of him everywhere. Why? What would these statues do for him? He wouldn't be able to see them. He wouldn't be able to enjoy these affirmations of his grandeur. He didn't even believe his soul would see them. Stalin needed his portrait all over the Soviet Union as well. People search for lasting fame, do all they can to feel special, different from the rest. Why?

It is all part of their need to create an illusion of being. Torah, on the other hand, teaches us that man's greatest drive is his need to achieve a true, meaningful existence.

Man has an unconscious awareness that he doesn't exist in an absolute sense; hence he searches, he struggles to become, even if only through an illusion. All of life represents his struggle to achieve real existence. All of creation is ephemeral, all existence contingent. In reality, we have no existence of our own at all. We are utterly contingent upon the will of our Creator. We are constantly being given existence by Him. Every second of our existence is a gift from the Almighty. He constantly renews our lives, as we read in our daily prayers, "He renews in His goodness, each day, continuously, the work of creation." We have no existence now simply because we existed a second ago. We exist now only because God is giving us existence this very moment.

The real wonder is that God grants us an accumulation of memories and prior consequences, as though there were any continuity with yesterday's existence. In reality, though, such a continuation does not exist: each moment is a new existence, literally a creation *ex nihilo*.

How is one granted this existence? Only by our connection to God, the only Source of existence. The closer we are to the Almighty, the more reality we achieve.

The basic drive of man is to achieve this reality through connecting with and cleaving to God. Man has a choice regarding this drive for a meaningful existence, as he has with all drives: he can harness it either to bring himself closer to God or to take himself farther away from Him. The need to experience existence may be manifested by striving to connect with the Source of all existence, the Almighty, or through various counterfeit means. For some people this drive is expressed in the struggle to attain power, while for others it is expressed in the striving for fame. The accumulation of wealth or approval is also a popular counterfeit outlet for this drive.

The Need to Serve

Life demands serving something. Man is part of creation, absolutely contingent upon the Almighty, and this dependency mandates a need to relate to something beyond himself. One can't escape this fact. However, these counterfeit means can only provide the illusion of existence.

There are endless ways to deal with this inescapable, fundamental human drive, but they all come down to this choice: one either serves God or serves idols. "Be careful lest your heart be misled and you turn aside and serve other gods."[1] "Turning aside" means straying from the Torah; once you stray from the Torah you will cleave to and serve idols.[2]

Why is this so? Is there no middle ground between straying from God and worshipping idols?

The Sages teach us that man needs to connect to the Almighty, to the Source of all existence. To achieve this connection, man must serve Him. If he does not serve God according to His revelation, he will inevitably go on to attach himself to some kind of idolatry. Just as the service of God provides meaning for man's existence, idolatry creates an illusion of meaning. When power, fame, wealth or ap-

---

1. Deuteronomy 11:16.

2. Rashi quoting *Sifri* on Deuteronomy 11:16.

proval becomes an end in itself, it is a form of idolatry. Idolatry can exist in communism, liberalism, atheism, or humanism. Man chooses either to connect to the Almighty by serving Him, or to create an illusion which he must serve. In matters of choice, there is no in-between.

The Meaning of Life

Either man relates to something, anything, greater than himself, or he attempts to lose himself and escape a meaningless reality. Technology has provided man with many opportunities to lose himself. How many hours are spent vicariously experiencing the pains and pleasures of others in front of the television or at the movies? How much money is spent on alcohol and other drugs by those who seek to avoid the confrontations of life? These escapes do not provide true happiness. They merely dull one's sensitivities to the pain that results when one does not relate to something beyond himself and his life is void of meaning.

Nothing to Worship

It is important to appreciate that the paramount consequence of not perceiving God as absolute is that it stifles man's urge to serve Him—it leaves nothing for one to truly worship.[3] If God is not absolute, then He is no more than a superman. The difference between man and God becomes quantitative, not qualitative. We are accustomed to a hierarchy of power. What if God is only more powerful than man, in a human, non-Divine sense? The president, too, is more powerful than we are, but we still feel we can evade him. Man can both avoid and manipulate anyone more powerful

---

3. Optimally, *avodah* (service or worship) implies fulfilling the Will of the Almighty out of love and a yearning to be close to the Source of all existence.

than himself; therefore, he would never serve such a being. For man to serve, to submit himself to supplicating God, the Almighty must be essentially different from him. The difference between God and man must be qualitative, not merely quantitative.

Idolatry as Barter

If this concept is true, then why do we find so many civilizations serving idols? The idol does not have any absolute existence, it has a contingent one. The idol, like those serving it, has needs and therefore limitations and weaknesses. Human awareness of this dependency invites relating to the idol through barter—service for a payoff. People will serve a god only as long as it offers some kind of benefit. Throughout history, the gods that were favored were those that were able to deliver the rains and victories that their worshippers desired. This form of worship, tit for tat, is self-serving and not sincere submission. The contingent existence of the idol is its inherent weakness, one that makes real submission to it impossible.

The recognition of the Almighty's absolute existence as the one and only Source of our existence is what binds us to Him. Submission to Him is predicated upon the knowledge that He is the Cause of the entire world and all the experience that one has within it. This knowledge, then, ultimately carries with it the profound realization that one has no absolute existence at all. It was out of this awareness that Moshe Rabbeinu declared:[4] "We, what are we?" To be aware that one is nothing more than God's creation and to be aware of all the ramifications of this reality is the highest expression of service.

---

4. Exodus 15:8; see *Chulin* 89a.

The Only Permanent Entity

Another consequence of the fact that God is absolute is the idea that He is unchanging. Contingent beings are affected by a variety of things and are constantly changing. One depends on something, and when that thing is altered, one must also change. God, who is not dependent upon anything and who has neither cause nor source other than His own Being, is unchanging.

The World to Come

The existence of a World to Come is predicated upon this first principle as well. What is the difference between this world and the World to Come? This world is ephemeral, transitory, like the blink of an eye. The World to Come is real, actual, and eternal. But the reality of the World to Come necessarily depends on God's absoluteness, on His non-contingency.

The Second Principle

God's Unity

We believe that this Primal Cause [God] is One. [His is] not like the oneness of a pair, nor like the oneness of a species, nor like man, whose complex oneness may be divided into many units, nor like the oneness of a simple body, which is one in number but may be divided and separated without end. Rather, He is One with a Oneness that knows no parallel in any manner. This is the second Principle, as affirmed by the verse (Deuteronomy 6:4) "Hear O Israel, God is our Lord, God is One."

The Second Principle

God's Unity

Existence Versus Unity

The second Principle of the Rambam is to "believe that this Primal Cause [God] is One," to appreciate the unity of Him who is the only source of power. This Oneness is absolute and unique, a Oneness that knows no parallel.

The first two Principles are actually two of the 613 commandments in the Torah: 1) to know the existence of God[5] and 2) to know the unity of God.[6] The presence of these two commandments presents a question. How could one possibly fulfill the first commandment, to know the existence of God, without knowing His Unity, the second commandment? The very notion of a Creator is, by definition, predicated upon the reality of His Oneness. The necessary logic of this idea

---

5. Rambam, *Mishneh Torah*, Laws of the Fundamentals of Torah 1:1-6.

6. Ibid., 1:7.

was clearly addressed in the first Principle, which stressed that the existence of God means His absolute existence, He being the only Source of reality.

It seems clear in the Rambam that one aspect of knowing God is knowing that He is the only source of power. Because he sees these two ideas as two interdependent concepts, it is therefore problematic that he lists them as two separate Principles. The Rambam believed that even though the second Principle can be inferred through and is an aspect of the first Principle, there is still a need to establish two separate Principles: the unity of God, as an aspect of His absolute nature, must be understood, articulated and integrated into one's approach to serving the Almighty.

The first Principle depicts the uniqueness of God in that He is absolutely independent of anything, in contrast to man, who is absolutely dependent upon Him. The second Principle emphasizes that everything we experience, the myriads of conflicting forces in our universe, reflects one Unity, a Oneness that knows no parallel. Pleasure and pain, joy and sorrow all have one Source. The good things that happen to bad people and the bad things that happen to good people all have one Origin.

The emphasis on God's Unity provided by this Principle rejects the subtle influences of polytheism which could exist even in a monotheistic system. Man has a tendency to identify good and evil, happiness and suffering, with separate causes, which creates the need for this Principle. One witnesses the various, seemingly conflicting facets of the Almighty's providence, and he is confused. It would be easy to resolve these contradictory elements of life by concluding that these facets represent separate, conflicting forces or powers controlling reality. This answer is the lure of polytheism, however. Seen more subtlely, in an effort to understand God's nature, monotheistic man incorrectly identifies with one aspect of the Almighty, such as His mercy, failing to appreciate His unity.

The fact that the Rambam has divided these concepts, the existence of God and the unity of God, into two Principles implies that one must specifically be aware and articulate both concepts in order to serve Him properly.

Let us consider a practical application of this Principle of the unity of God. It is a given that any small country can make its living by playing off the United States politically and economically against the U.S.S.R. The tactics of extorting aid under the threat of joining the other side are familiar in world politics. Individuals as well, with a little finesse, can become quite adept at playing off a person against himself. One manipulates, for example, a person's desire for prestige against his desire for money. The con artist has the situation all worked out. He asks himself, what does my victim value more— people praising his role in a cause and proclaiming how wonderful he is, or his money? He then focuses upon the various strengths and weaknesses of the victim's personality and merely plays one against the other.

Most people are not willing to expend the time and energy to play this game with peers. But when it comes to God, if there would not be this absolute unity, then we would be trying to con Him all the time. People would find ways to rationalize their actions by appealing to another characteristic, another side of Him. Whether it would be His mercy against His meting out of justice, or His loving-kindness against His might, people would attempt to evade His wrath and His authority by relating to an alternative aspect of His Being. However, since His Unity is absolute, we must always deal with His totality. God cannot be manipulated by playing off one of His traits against another in order to justify actions.

This failure to appreciate God's Unity can manifest itself in even subtler ways. Our Sages say that Noah's faith was deficient. In their words:[7] "Noah also was among those people who are wanting in faith. He believed and he did not believe that the Flood would come." How is this statement possible? Didn't Noah labor 120 years, despite ridicule and persecution, to build the ark? His hostile world tried to destroy him with every means available and only by the grace of God did he survive. It is obvious that he endured this harassment because he was following God's instructions, because of his faith in God. How then is it possible to accuse Noah of being "wanting in faith"?

The question becomes more complicated when we consider that Noah was a prophet and communicated directly with the Almighty, thereby leaving less room for doubt within his faith. To charge a prophet with a lack of faith doesn't seem possible. How could a prophet doubt the word of God?

The answer to this question of faltering faith lies in the fact that the Sages were calling our attention to a flaw in Noah's appreciation of the unity of God. Actually, he never doubted that the Almighty could destroy the world. He never doubted the word of God. Yet, because there existed an imperfection in his perception of God's Oneness, Noah trusted that the mercy of the Creator would overwhelm His trait of justice.

---

7. Bereishis Rabbah 32:9.

The Third Principle

God's Incorporeality

We believe that this Oneness is neither a body nor a bodily force, nor is He subject to any bodily characteristics—movement, rest, or dwelling—be they inherent or by chance. Therefore the Sages, may their memory be blessed, repudiated [the possibility of any] cohesion or separation [concerning Him], as they said: "Above there is no sitting, standing, division, or 'cohesion' " (a usage based on Isaiah 11:14). As the prophet (ibid., 40:18-25) said: "Who is comparable to the Almighty...?" For if He had a body, He could be compared to other bodies.

All the corporeal terms used in the Scriptures to describe Him—such as walking, standing, sitting, speaking, etc.—are metaphorical. As the Sages have said: "The Torah speaks in the language of man." The Sages have already dealt with this subject extensively.

This is the third Principle, as affirmed by the verse (Deuteronomy 4:15) "You have not seen any image," that is to say, you cannot conceive of Him as having any form because, as stated, He is neither a body nor a bodily force.

The Third Principle

God's Incorporeality

The Limitations of Time and Space

It is necessary to understand and be aware of God's incorporeality because if God occupied space, man could be free of Him. If God occupied space, He would be limited and He would have boundaries. A physical being cannot be in two places at the same time. If the Almighty were limited in space, then man could elude His awareness. If man could elude His awareness, then God could no longer tell humanity how to act. When an individual felt like doing something wrong, he could make sure that it was dark, that he was hidden, and that he had thus escaped, smug in his confidence that God would never find out.

If one believes that God is physical, he will feel capable of escaping Him. One need not intellectually follow this logical reasoning to reach this conclusion: a human being will naturally act out the logical consequences of the concepts he believes. A man does not have to be a philosopher in order to realize these logical consequences. Without considering, he instinctively reacts from the position of his beliefs. If he takes the position that God is corporeal, that He occupies space, then he will intuitively conclude that he can hide from Him.

The Raavad[8] disagrees with the ramifications of believing that God is corporeal. He believes that man can avoid the logical consequences of his beliefs. If an individual believes that God is corporeal, he is making a significant mistake, but he can still relate to the Almighty and still be bound by His Torah. He may not feel able to escape God, even though this feeling is the logical consequence of his belief.

Spiritual and Material

Although the concept of God's incorporeality is generally understood, the parallel concept of His non-spirituality is not well known. Although God is frequently referred to as a spiritual Being, we apply the term loosely for lack of another word. If a material object is defined as being confined to time and space, while something spiritual is confined in terms of time but not in terms of space, then it must be concluded that God is neither physical nor spiritual. The Almighty is confined neither in space nor in time. All material and spiritual beings were created by Him, as it is written:[9] "In the beginning God created the heavens and the earth." Our Sages learned that "the heavens" is a reference to spiritual creations, such as the angels and the "Throne of Honor", while "the earth" refers to all material existence. The souls of men, also spiritual entities, were likewise created. Thus, it is incorrect to describe God in spiritual terms. He is unique, neither physical nor spiritual, the Creator of both the physical and the spiritual worlds.

---

8. Rambam, *Mishneh Torah*, Laws of Repentance 3:7.
9. Genesis 1:1.

The verse which the Rambam cites as proof of God's incorporeality can also be applied to His non-spirituality. He quotes the prophet Isaiah:[10] "Who is comparable to the Almighty?" If God were material, He could be compared to everything material in creation. In the same manner, if He were spiritual, then He could be compared to anything spiritual in creation. Neither comparison can be made, for there is no relationship of any kind that could describe Him in any way other than by what is implied by His being the Creator. We can understand Him only in terms of the Creator-creation relationship.

Yet the Rambam's third Principle deals only with God's incorporeality. Why doesn't it include the aspect of His non-spirituality? What is the difference between the significance of His incorporeality and the significance of His non-spirituality?

As we have defined the Rambam's conception of the Principles, the answer to this question depends on whether lack of awareness of God's non-spirituality may actually preclude one's serving Him. As has been discussed, the Thirteen Principles are the fundamental concepts which are absolutely essential in order for man to relate correctly to the Almighty and His Torah.

As mentioned earlier, one who perceives God as a corporeal entity, limited in time and space, can and will ultimately feel that He can be avoided. The consequence of this error translates into the belief that man is not bound by the Torah. The lack of awareness of God's non-spirituality, on the other hand, does not bear similar consequences. His being spiritual or not does not affect our orientation in terms of being able to escape Him or serve Him. Because our orientation is not affected, the issue of spirituality is not included in this Principle.

---

10. Isaiah 40:18, 25.

The Fourth Principle

Ex Nihilo

We believe that this Oneness is necessarily primary. All that exists other than Him is not primary in relationship to Him. There are many references to this in the Scriptures. This is the fourth Principle, as affirmed by the verse (Deuteronomy 33:27) "God who preceded [all existence] is a refuge...."

The Fourth Principle

Ex Nihilo

More than Eternity

Ani Ma'amin, an abridged version of the Thirteen Principles written by an unknown author, reads, "I believe with
complete faith that the Creator, blessed be His name, is the
first and the last." The point of this statement seems to be
that God has no beginning and no end; He exists outside of
time and is therefore not limited by it. Thus, the statement in
Ani Ma'amin appears to be a repetition of the first Principle
of absolute existence, which, by definition, means that He
has no beginning and no end. If He suddenly sprang into
existence, He would be dependent upon the source that
brought Him into being. As discussed in the examination of
the first Principle, it is impossible to conceive of God as an
absolute being from which everything else derives unless He
Himself has no beginning.

By adding the idea of eternity, *Ani Ma'amin* is misleading. It implies that the Rambam is referring to God existing

outside of time. A careful reading of the Rambam, however, shows that this implication is incorrect. Instead, the Rambam is actually presenting the idea that the Almighty preceded the universe and created it *ex nihilo*. This is evident from the verse he cites:[11] "God who preceded all existence is a refuge...." The Principle is not that "He was the first", a statement which implies that He may have had a beginning; rather, He was "without a beginning", the absolute first: He preceded all Existence and created all Existence from a perfect void.

The Eternity of Matter

This Principle of creation *ex nihilo* has been the subject of a classic dispute among philosophers throughout history. In his *Guide for the Perplexed*,[12] the Rambam states that it would be possible (though wrong) to accept the story of Creation in Genesis while still assuming that matter was eternal. This concept of the eternity of matter implies that God and the universe co-existed without any beginning, an idea held by Aristotle. The Greek philosopher acknowledged a god as creator, but insisted that just as its existence had no beginning and no end, its role as a creator had no beginning and no end. Consequently, its creation had no beginning and no end. To Aristotle, the eternity of matter was not a contradiction to his belief that God was the Source of all Existence.

Aristotle's Powerless God

It is with this Principle that the Rambam parts company with Aristotle. The god of Aristotle is merely a docile machine. It cannot choose to act or react. It is what it is. It

---

11. Deuteronomy 33:27.
12. Vol. 2, ch. 25.

could not and cannot choose to become Creator. It is impotent, with no understanding, no awareness and no freedom. Such a god, so limited, cannot be served. In contrast, the Rambam's God preceded Creation and is free to choose to create. He observes and controls. The world is His. Aristotle's god has no control; even man has more control than Aristotle's god. It is bound by its own nature and therefore has no relationship with creation. None of the names of God that describe Him as He relates to creation would be applicable to the god of Aristotle. It is neither a Lord nor a Master nor a Power. In Aristotle's world, there is nothing to serve because it is impossible to serve a limited force.

A Leap of Faith

This Principle of creation *ex nihilo* we know only from the Torah. Both the Rambam[13] and Yehudah HaLevi[14] admit that it is impossible to prove Aristotle wrong through logic. Up until this point in our discussion, intellect acted as a guide to considering the truth of each of these Principles, step by step. Since Aristotle cannot be proven wrong by logic, we must now rely on God's revelation to Israel in order to know the truth.

It would seem, however, that this Principle could be derived through reason as well. Wasn't that what happened in our history with the story of Abraham? Didn't he look at the "palace"[15] and understand that there had to be an Owner? He observed the universe and knew there had to be a Creator. Not only did Abraham perceive a God who creates, but he also concluded that this Creator cares for and imposes obligations upon creation. With total clarity and an extraordinary

---

13. *Guide for the Perplexed*, ch. 16.

14. *Kuzari*, 1:63-67.

15. *Midrash HaGadol* 12:1; *Bereishis Rabbah* 39:1.

fidelity to his convictions, he deduced all these facts to the extent that he was willing to give his life for this Creator. In order to be willing to be thrown into the burning furnace rather than worship idols,[16] he had to understand that there was a system of morality that came from a Creator. This system of morality defined the relationship between the Creator and man to the extent that it was proper and necessary to defend the truth even at the cost of life itself.

With his intellect, Abraham saw in the universe a God far different from the impotent, mechanical god of Aristotle. The God of Abraham related to man in such a way that man could address Him as "my Lord, my Master."[17] One might say that the inference of a caring God from the perfect design of the universe is a subtle step that demands *trust* as well as logic.

To Aristotle the "why" of Creation ·must remain a mystery. Obviously, the world was not created in order to fulfill the needs of the Creator, because by definition He lacks nothing, He has no needs. If, according to Aristotle, creating is part of the very definition of the Creator, then there never existed a separate act of Creation or a separate will on the part of the Creator to create.

In Aristotle's terms there never existed an act of giving, of *chesed*, such that one could term Creation an act of giving to the created; the question of "why" in Creation does not exist. Avraham, on the other hand, could not leave this "why" unresolved. To him the sublime order of the universe testified to purpose and meaning. This conviction led him to conclude that the Almighty was not always a Creator. He became convinced that God willed Creation for the benefit of the created and, specifically, for the benefit of man. This

---

16. *Bereishis Rabbah* 38:19.

17. Genesis 15:2; see *Berachos* 7b.

benefit is the absolute pleasure that is derived from closeness to the Source of all existence. The more man would emulate the Creator, the closer he could come to Him. Since Abraham came to know God through a Divine attribute manifested in Creation—that of *chesed*, of giving—it follows that the theme of Abraham's life became one of giving to others.

The Fifth Principle

The Service of God

He [God], may He be blessed, is the only One whom it is proper to serve [worship], to praise, to make known His grandeur, and to fulfill His commandments. This should not be done to any entity that is subservient to Him, be it the angels, the stars, the planets, or the elements or their compounds. For their activity is programmed. They have no control, and no choice but to perform His will. Thus it is improper to serve them as intermediaries in order to come close to God. Rather, one should direct his thoughts toward the Almighty alone and abandon anything other than Him. This is the fifth Principle, warning us against idolatry, as affirmed throughout the Torah.

The Fifth Principle

The Service of God

Who Wields Power

In order to understand the fifth Principle, concerning the worship of the Almighty exclusively, it is important to differentiate between a source of power and a wielder of power. To the intelligent mind the idea of idolatry is not in terms of the source of power but more in terms of the wielder of power.

The military can serve as a good example of the difference between the two. A sergeant is a wielder of power. However, in terms of the source of power, he is low in the hierarchy. His power is ultimately derived from the president, the commander in chief. Although the president is the source of power, he is not the wielder of power for the average serviceman.

It doesn't make any difference to the soldier how far removed the sergeant is from the source of power. As long as the sergeant is the one who decides whether the soldier receives a weekend pass, or what type of work he has to do, it is the sergeant whom the soldier is concerned with pleasing. The sergeant then is the wielder of power, while the president is the source of power. Where the sergeant's power is derived from makes no difference to the serviceman. As far as he is concerned, he serves only the sergeant.

God in the Image of Man

In the same way, idolatry generally concerns itself with the wielder of power rather than with the Source of power. In the eyes of idolators, the idol was seen neither as the source of their existence nor as the source of their well-being. They understood that ultimately there was a god who was the source of their existence, but they thought that he had delegated power in much the same way as the president delegates power to the sergeant. In this situation, man imagines a god delegating authority so that it might be able to concentrate on, so to speak, higher policies. Thus, when man creates his own image of God, he inevitably creates a god in the image of man.

As the Rambam explains,[18] originally everyone believed that God was the only Source of power. Unfortunately, the generation of Enosh began to speculate that since God created heavenly bodies and placed them in high positions, it was obviously His will that man honor them. Initially, these people understood that the heavenly bodies had no power of their own, but because they believed that God intended the heavenly bodies to be served, mankind fell into the belief that the endowment of this honor signified that these bodies actually had power.

---

18. Rambam, *Mishneh Torah*, Laws of Idolatry 1:1.

Power and Freedom

The words of the Rambam make this relationship between power and freedom of choice quite explicit:[19] "[God] is the only One whom it is proper to serve [worship], to praise, to make known His grandeur, and to fulfill His commandments. This should not be done to any entity that is subservient to Him, be it the angels, the stars, the planets, or the elements or their compounds. For their activity is programmed. They have no control, and no choice but to perform His will."

No created being but man has free will. All other beings are "programmed". To ask anything of them demonstrates that one is attributing power to them, which is the essence of idolatry. To ask the angels to take your prayers to God, thinking that they have a choice regarding whether to take your prayers or not to take them, is idolatry. Similarly, asking an angel to bless you, thinking that it can choose whether to bless you or not, is idolatry.[20] The Almighty uses the angels

---

19. Rambam, *Commentary to the Mishnah, Sanhedrin* 10:1.

20. It is a form of idolatry to attribute power or free will to any intermediary. Therefore, believing that one must beg angels to bring his prayers to God is idolatry. For this reason, the Maharal and Rav Chaim of Volozhin (*Keser Rosh,* no. 93) forbade the singing of "*Barchuni leshalom,*" since it implies that one is asking the angels to bless him.

Those who do sing this popular prayer on the Sabbath should envision a situation in which the angels will *have* to bless him. The Talmud (*Shabbos* 119b) relates that, returning home after the Sabbath services Friday evening, one is accompanied by two angels. If, upon entering one's home, the angels find the table set for the Sabbath meal, they are forced to bless the home with the blessing that this joy and preparation should occur the following week as well. It is for this situation, where the angels must bless him, that one should pray.

to relate to tasks not worthy of being dealt with directly by Him. They are like programmed mechanical hands assisting in the production of cars in an assembly line. They are the means by which God maintains His distance from those who have not merited His direct intimacy.

Only God and man have free will. For this reason, one cannot bow down to an angel but can bow to a man. For example, one can beg a doctor to take someone as his patient since the doctor has power and can refuse to help. Therefore, David cries:[21] "Let us fall into God's hands for His mercies are abundant, but let me not fall into human hands." Although man's free will cannot affect a perfectly righteous man, it can and does affect those who are not perfectly righteous. The criteria that influence the decision of the Almighty not to intervene to prevent man's actions are different from those which influence His decision to punish someone. In a situation where His "patience" would give someone time to repent and mend his ways, He may decide not to intervene to protect that individual from the potential harm caused by his fellow man.

On the other hand, although "everything is in the hands of God,"[22] man can influence the manner in which God rewards and punishes. This situation illustrates that man has power. We see the manifestation of this power with Abraham. God "descended"[23] to consult Abraham about the impending destruction of Sodom, giving him a chance to influence Divine Judgment. Having this power to influence, man shares the title "elohim" with the Almighty.[24] Because he has this influence, he and only he of all the creation can be bribed through gifts, money, or power. The power man has and all

---

21. II Samuel 24:14.
22. Berachos 33b.
23. Genesis 18:21.
24. Rashi on Exodus 22:7.

its ramifications result from the reality of man's free will.

Exercising Free Will—Even While Denying It

The free will of man is the foundation of the Torah. The Rambam discusses the concept of free will at length in the *Mishneh Torah* within the Laws of Repentance.[25] Even so, this concept is not considered in any of the Principles. Apparently, the Rambam feels that it is not necessary for man to be consciously aware of the fact that he has free will when he approaches the mitzvos. Without such an awareness, one can still be a practicing Jew.

Philosophers who debate whether there is such a thing as free will are just playing a game, says the Rambam. Even as they debate, they are making decisions and choices. They can contemplate all they want as to whether or not they are making a choice, but the fact remains that they are using their free will. They react to the world as if they had free will; they become angry at those who hurt them and acknowledge those who please them; they won't elect anyone they feel is evil or corrupt; they denounce Hitler, although without free will there is no difference between Hitler and Mother Teresa. In every aspect of their lives they exercise and recognize free will, even if they deny that they do.

Since the ability to utilize our free will is instinctively with us, as illustrated above, there is no need to include it as an additional Principle. The intention of the Rambam was to include only those tenets of faith of which knowledge and awareness are absolutely necessary in order to relate to the Torah. Utilization of these tenets is not instinctive, unlike man's free will. Nevertheless, the Rambam discusses the concept of free will in the *Mishneh Torah* in order to remind us not to join in the game of those who attempt to deny it, and

25. Ch. 5.

not to join those destructive elements of society whose hidden agenda involves portraying a mechanical universe where all events are caused and preconditioned. Essentially, the idea of such a universe relieves man of all responsibility, which explains why seemingly intelligent people are willing to indulge in such fantasies.

The Great Gift of God

The concept of free will is very deep and profound. Without it there would exist only the power of the Creator and, as a result, the entire universe would be impotent and passive. By giving man free will, God endowed him with power so that two forces would exist in the universe. As a result of this endowment, it became possible to have a covenant between the Creator and creation. It became possible to have commandments and a relationship with God, both of which are meaningless without man's free will. We have free will only because God grants us this magnificent gift.

On the other hand, in examining the story of Pharaoh in Egypt,[26] we can understand that just as He grants man this free will, He can also deny it when man no longer deserves it. Because of the evil that Pharaoh had perpetrated, God "hardened his heart," taking away his free will in order to use him as a pawn in history.[27]

The greatest paradox of existence is therefore the independence which the Almighty gives to a totally dependent creature. This gift is the immeasurable kindness the Sages speak of when they describe how the Almighty gives man the strength and intelligence to rebel against Him. A comparable situation would involve a government that supplies rebels with the guns, ammunition, clothing, and food with

---

26. Exodus 1-14.
27. Rambam, *Mishneh Torah*, Laws of Repentance 6:3.

which to carry on a revolution. The gift of free will is such an act of loving-kindness, because without the potential to rebel, man could never come close to his Creator. A covenant, a treaty necessitates the participation of both parties. It can never be unilateral. The uniqueness of the Jewish Nation, the relationship that is based upon a covenant between the Jew and God, would not be possible without free will. That relationship, which was the purpose of Creation, and that pleasure—the greatest of all pleasures—would be denied man.

To attribute free will to anything else in the creation inevitably leads to idolatry. If one would come to believe that an angel has the choice of granting or not granting a favor, he would be tempted, after pleading with the angel, to bring him a little gift to persuade him. Thus, the Rambam appropriately states that this Principle of serving only God is supported by all the admonitions against idolatry in the Torah.

Part II
Direct Communication
Between Man and God

The Sixth Principle

Prophecy

Man should know that there are men of great ability and perfection whose souls are primed to receive pure intellectual form. Their human intellect cleaves to this active intellect and receives a profound emanation. These [men] are prophets and this [process] is prophecy. To explain this Principle with clarity would be lengthy and our intention is neither to adduce proofs for each Principle nor to present a complete elaboration of each, for this would encompass all wisdom. We are merely enumerating the Principles. Numerous verses in the Torah attest to the prophecy of our many prophets.

The Sixth Principle

Prophecy

The first Principle of this series is to be aware of and to accept fully the fact that God communicates with human beings. The Rambam describes the experience of prophecy in the following manner:[1] "The information that is made known to the prophet in a prophetic vision is made known through a parable whose meaning is immediately engraved [understood] in his heart in such a manner that he knows what it is." It is clear from this statement that the source of the communication is external. There is no way for man to discover the will of God other than through direct communication of this nature.

The Rambam's choice of the term "prophecy" rather than "inspiration" is significant:

Prophecy is defined as the reality of man receiving a direct

---

1. Rambam, *Mishneh Torah*, Laws of the Fundamentals of Torah 7:3.

and clear message from God. In terms of Torah, prophecy involves receiving the actual words of the Almighty. In terms of the Prophets, however, prophecy involves receiving a vision, a mental image, with its exact interpretation. In both cases, a clear, distinct message emanates from God and is perceived by man.

Inspiration, on the other hand, may emanate from God, in which case it is Divine inspiration, or it may come from within, from man himself. Because of the latter possibility, inspiration could never be the basis of the Torah. When being inspired, one may easily confuse the source of his inspiration. In examining history, how many madmen have been inspired? Aren't Gadaffi and Arafat inspired? Doesn't their inspiration form the basis of their peoples' ideology?

The difference between Divine inspiration and Divine prophecy is in the manner in which the *hashgachah*, or Divine providence, manifests itself. To one who is Divinely inspired, the *hashgachah* of the Almighty provides guidance in his endeavors; to the prophet who receives Divine prophecy, the *hashgachah* of the Almighty provides a clear message.

Those contemporary thinkers who believe that the Torah was not given through direct communication with the Almighty, that the words of Torah are not His exact words but merely the Divinely inspired words of men, do humanity a great disservice. Their claim that the Torah is only a product of Divine inspiration is convenient. Since a person is easily inspired by messages he wants to hear, a law built upon inspiration obviously will not command the respect and authority necessary to bind man; rather, it will become malleable in his hands. Such a Torah would cease to be the source of life from Above, and would instead become a mere product of and target for human manipulation.

The Seventh Principle

The Prophecy of Moshe Rabbeinu

*We believe that [Moshe Rabbeinu] is the father
of all the prophets before and after him, all of
whom were beneath him in stature. He was
chosen above all mankind, achieving a greater
knowledge of the Almighty than anyone before
or since. Moshe Rabbeinu reached a level that
surpasses human attainment and approximates
the angelic. There was no barrier that he did not
penetrate, no physical limitation that hindered
him, and no imperfection large or small [to impede
him]. In achieving this [level], he lost his sensual
and imaginative faculties; his drives and desires
ceased, leaving only his pure intellect. Concerning this it is said that Moshe communicated with
God without any angelic intermediary.*

The Seventh Principle

The Prophecy of Moshe Rabbeinu

The Unchanging Torah

In essence, this principle establishes the fact that the Torah cannot be altered. In order for man to be able to serve God, it is necessary to know His Will in absolute, unchanging terms and to recognize it as such. Any room for change will create the opportunity for man to inject his own values. When the possibility of change exists, man's priorities and convenience dominate, making him a servant of himself rather than his Creator.

Fortunately, the authority of the Torah itself prevents man from tampering with it. The unparalleled circumstances and content of the prophecy of Moshe Rabbeinu, together with the historically unique revelation of the Torah on Sinai, provide the basis for that authority. One of the laws revealed there through Moshe states that nothing can ever be added or subtracted from the Torah that God gave, word for word, to Moshe Rabbeinu.[2] Even a prophet cannot claim the right to innovate anything in the Torah. He can never carry an authentic message from God proposing revision of any detail in the Torah.

Father of Prophets

To begin to understand the limitations of the other prophets, we must appreciate the difference between their revelations and those of Moshe Rabbeinu. The Rambam begins this Principle by stating, "Moshe Rabbeinu is the father of all the prophets before and after him." What does he mean? How can Moshe be the father of Abraham, who lived hundreds of years before him? Although the Rambam elaborates upon the various differences between the prophecies of Moshe Rabbeinu and the other prophets, these differences are not the essence of the Principle. The essence, that which must be realized by each Jew, is that Moshe Rabbeinu is the "father of all the prophets," which means that he is the *source* of the authority for all prophecy.

Mass Revelation

The Rambam can only be understood through appreciating the uniqueness of the Sinaitic experience, that which differentiates the Jewish faith from all others. All the religions in the world, except for Judaism, have one thing in common. They all require one to surrender his mind, to take a leap of faith in order to adhere to their beliefs. As long as one is thinking critically, he might well come to reject these religions. For every religion that mankind has invented is dependent upon the testimony of no more than a few individuals. In terms of the pursuit of truth, such evidence is far from satisfactory. The literature of these religions frequently describes a leap of faith, a nice way of saying that one may only

---

2. Deuteronomy 13:1.

progress through ignoring his critical, intellectual facilities.

The difference between the revelations and major prophets of other religions and those of Judaism may be illustrated by a story the Jews have told for hundreds of years:

A great Rebbe died, survived by his two sons. However, he left no instructions as to which son was to inherit the mantel of leadership in the community. The congregation itself was equally divided between the two. Some insisted that one son was more qualified while others were sure that the other son would be the better Rebbe. After weeks, the conflict finally came to a standstill, since the elders of the community could not decide who should be their new Rebbe.

Then, one day, one of the sons approached the Council of Elders and told them an amazing story. He insisted that his father, the Rebbe, had come to him in a dream the night before, and had told him to convey to the elders his command that this son become their new Rebbe.

Upon hearing this story, a hush fell over the Council. Would this new development settle at last the dispute that had occupied the minds and mouths of the whole community for so long? Was this what they had been waiting for?

As the suspense grew, a little old man who was sitting in the corner, amused at what he'd heard, softly decided the matter: "Young man, if your father, the Rebbe, had wanted you to be the new leader of our community, he should have come to *us* in *our* dreams, not to *you* in *yours*."

In the same way, logically, if God wanted to appoint a prophet to communicate His Will to a people, He would not reveal Himself to the prophet alone, instructing *him* to tell the people that he had been chosen by God as their prophet. Instead, He would reveal directly to the *people* His desire that this individual be His prophet.

Of all the religions that have been started throughout history, there exists only one where this situation occurred. Only in giving the Torah on Mount Sinai did God appear to an entire nation. The revelation at Sinai was experienced neither by an individual nor by a chosen group of individuals, but by an entire nation—men, women and children. The Almighty, so to speak, begs man:[3] "Ask, now: of the earliest days that were before you, since the day that God created man upon the earth, and from one end of the heaven to the other end, has there ever been such a great thing as this or was there ever heard anything like it? Has a nation heard the voice of God...?"

In looking at the pages of history, one sees that the story of Sinai was original and has never been repeated. Not only has it never happened again, but no one has even tried to create and tell such a story. The attempt has never been made because it is impossible to make up a story of this nature. In examining great world literature, we find that every plot has its parallels in the various cultures. Certainly, such a story, one that has captured the minds and imaginations of so many people, that serves as the basis of three major religions, would have been copied if this were at all possible. But just as the Rebbe's son did not dare tell the Council of Elders that his father appeared to *them* in a dream, humanity has never dared to tell of God appearing to any nation other than the Jews. If the invention of such a story would be possible, it would have been imitated many, many times; one just can't invent such a story and get away with it.

No Need to Make the Leap of Faith

The Jewish Nation did not only believe in God—it also knew and experienced Him. For this reason, basing itself on objective evidence—the testimony of three million eye-

---

3. Deuteronomy 4:32.

witnesses—Judaism does not need to demand a leap of faith. Just as the Almighty gave us our hearts and our emotions to use in order to serve Him, He also gave us our minds. In contrast, a leap of faith demands that an individual not use his intellect in serving God; rather, he should "just have faith".

In the same way, Moshe Rabbeinu is the only prophet in history whose authenticity was attested to, publicly, by God Himself. He is the only prophet appointed in the presence of an entire nation. He is the only prophet who was made known as such to his followers, rather than being accepted on "blind faith". Subsequently, any other prophet merits credibility only through the authority of Moshe Rabbeinu. The validity of their prophecies is based upon the definition which Moshe told the Jewish people God provided as to when an individual should be accepted by the nation as a prophet.

Since a prophet's credibility is based upon the criteria revealed through Moshe Rabbeinu, the Rambam refers to Moshe as "the father of all prophets." Thus, the world knows that Avraham was a prophet only because Moshe Rabbeinu testified—in the name of the Almighty, as it were—that God spoke to the father of the Jewish People. The world knows that Isaiah was a prophet only because he fulfilled all of the requirements that Moshe Rabbeinu communicated to the nation, in the name of God, concerning the status of a prophet.

Therefore, all prophets are prophets only through the testimony of Moshe Rabbeinu, the father of all prophets. It would be absurd even to consider the words of anyone who claims to be a prophet while proceeding to contradict any-thing in the Torah, for he is clearly undermining the very source of his supposed credibility.

In summation, the essence of this Principle is that aware-ness of the uniqueness of the revelation of Moshe Rabbeinu translates into the realization and law that Torah cannot and will not under any circumstances be changed.

Different Types of Prophecy

The sixth Principle states that Torah is, *word for word*, the words of the Almighty. All other prophecy, on the other hand, is given to a prophet through a mental image, a precise interpretation of which he is empowered and allowed to transmit. The Torah explicitly states that there are specific differences between the type of prophecy of Moshe Rab-beinu and that of all other prophets. It is these differences which distinguish Torah from the Prophets.

In order to further understand the difference between them, it is helpful to elaborate upon this idea that the Torah not only contains different material from a different period, it also represents a significant difference in the very method of communication.

To begin with, it is important to note that the Torah includes not only the prophecy of Moshe Rabbeinu but the entire Jewish Nation's prophecy at Mount Sinai. At the moment the Revelation began, the Jewish Nation achieved a level of prophecy similar to that of Moshe Rabbeinu.[4] The people themselves heard the words: "I, God am to be your God, who brought you out of the land of Egypt, out of the house of slaves."[5] Every single member of the People of Israel

---

4. See Seforno on Exodus 19:9, 11. There was always some doubt within the Jewish Nation as to whether God had indeed spoken face to face with Moshe without any medium, and while he was in command of his senses, until the people themselves experienced this level of prophecy at Sinai. Before this revelation, the entire Na-tion had to purify itself and abstain from marital relations.

5. Exodus 20:3.

heard these words and experienced the beginning of the prophecy that would prove to be unique to Moshe Rabbeinu. None of the other prophets experienced prophecy of this nature. No other prophet, other than Moshe Rabbeinu, heard the prophecy he transmitted, word for word, directly from the Almighty. Every single word, from "In the beginning God created the heavens and the earth"[6] until "in all the great awesomeness which Moshe had achieved before the eyes of all Israel,"[7] is the word of God. Moshe Rabbeinu was a mere transcriber, the instrument through which these words reached us.

The Sages tell us,[8] "No two prophets have the same style." One can refer to the "style" of the prophets because they themselves worded the thoughts that were communicated to them through the visions they saw. Although an interpretation was included with their vision, the words were the words of the prophets. Nonetheless, the Almighty assured the Jews that they were receiving an accurate interpretation of these visions.

There must exist a different mode of prophecy for communicating word for word in comparison to the transmission of concepts and thoughts. It is this difference that the Torah itself postulates when it testifies to Moshe's uniqueness as a prophet:[9] "And no prophet arose since, in Israel, like Moshe, whom the Almighty knew face to face."

Aspects of the Difference

The Rambam elaborates upon several major aspects of the uniqueness of Moshe Rabbeinu's prophecy in this Principle:

---

6. Genesis 1:1.

7. Deuteronomy 34:12.

8. *Sanhedrin* 89a.

9. Deuteronomy 34:10.

1) Every prophet [other than Moshe] experienced prophecy only while sleeping, as it is said in various places: "in a nighttime dream,"[10] "in a nighttime dream-vision,"[11] and many other [quotes] such as these. Alternatively, [the experience of prophecy was] during the day, after [the prophet] had fallen into a deep trance, so that all his senses were nullified and his thoughts remained free, as in a dream. This [occurrence] is called a "vision" or a "revelation", as is said, "in the revelations of God."[12]

[However, concerning] Moshe, the word of the Almighty came to him during the day, as he was standing between the two cherubim, as God attested: "I will meet with you there and I will speak to you from above the curtain, from between the two cherubim which are upon the ark of the testimony,"[13] and as He said, "if he were one of your prophets I, God, would reveal Myself to him in a vision, in a dream would I speak to him. Not so My servant Moshe: in the whole of My house he is trustworthy. Mouth to mouth I speak to him...."[14]

2) When a prophet receives prophecy, even though it is through a vision and an intermediary, his strength fails him, his body becomes shattered, and an awesome fear falls upon him, so that his soul almost departs from him...[but concerning] Moshe, it was not so. The word came to him and he was not overwhelmed with confusion or fear in any manner....

3) With all the prophets, the presence of prophecy rested upon them not whenever they chose but according to the Will of the Almighty. The prophet could [therefore] wait many days and years and not receive prophecy. He could ask

---

10. Genesis 31:24.
11. Job 33:15.
12. Ezekiel 8:3.
13. Exodus 25:22.
14. Numbers 12:6-8.

the Almighty to communicate a specific matter to him through prophecy, and wait many days or months until he received it, or he could never receive it. There were many groups of them [prophets] who prepared themselves and purified their thoughts, as Elisha did, as it says, "And now bring me a minstrel,"[15] and then the prophecy came to him. [But they] would not necessarily receive prophecy every time [they] prepared themselves. But whenever Moshe Rabbeinu desired [to communicate with God], he said [to the People of Israel]: "Wait, and I will hear what God will command you."[16]

Here, the Rambam has indicated significant qualitative differences between the prophecies of Moshe Rabbeinu and of all other prophets. His prophetic superiority has two implications:

First of all, the man himself was truly greater than all other prophets—they are secondary to him. Moshe was in control of himself physically and emotionally during his prophecies, while all other prophets lost control in the presence of God. Their physical functioning was suspended while in their prophetic trance. It seems that they had to "leave their bodies" in order for their minds and souls to receive God's message. Moshe Rabbeinu, however, was able to function normally and lucidly while in the presence of the Almighty. He was able to hear words directly from God, whereas all other prophets could only receive His messages in a metaphor or riddle. True, they also received the interpretation of the metaphor, but not in the actual words of God. Moshe's prophetic superiority is, in itself, reason that his words cannot be contradicted by any other prophet.

Second, the prophecy of Moshe Rabbeinu—which was

15. II Kings 3:15.
16. Numbers 9:8.

validated through a unique moment in history, the revelation to the entire Nation of Israel—that prophecy is Torah. "Torah" *presents* the absolute truths of the Almighty directly communicated to man. Thus, learning Torah is the closest a human can come to acquiring an intimate knowledge of God.

In contrast, the prophecy of all other prophets is not Torah. Indeed, their prophecy is validated only through the criteria established by Torah. However, since the revelation at Sinai will never be repeated (see the ninth Principle), prophecy of this type, for all of humanity other than the generation that witnessed Sinai, represents the ultimate religious experience.

Prophecy is the culmination of a lifetime of trying to come close to God. In the vast majority of situations, it was a gift from the Almighty, bestowed upon a righteous scholar who had diligently toiled to become worthy of it. In certain cases, prophecy was granted in order to deliver a message to a community or the Nation. These messages served as a source of insight or inspiration regarding the teachings of the Torah, or else they shed light upon current events, or warned of future happenings. However, these communications *never* innovated any Torah commandment.

Changing Commandments

A prophet has no right to innovate or change any law of the Torah. For this reason, the easiest way to spot a false prophet is to examine whether the content of his communication contradicts Torah. How could one accept any other prophecy over Torah? As discussed, the prophecy of "the father of all prophets" was unique, requiring no leap of faith or trust in an individual.

The difference between Moshe's prophecy, the Torah,

and other prophecy is based upon this seventh Principle, that the Torah cannot be changed. As stated, if it were possible to amend the Torah, there would be "prophets" constantly seeking to replace previous revelations with their own. Consequently, there would be no way to maintain the Torah. It would not be absolute.

One can appreciate the importance of this Principle by speculating: what would be the first commandment to be affected if a later prophecy could change the Torah? Would it be Shabbos or *kashrus?* The Sages, with their profound understanding of the nature of man, suggested that those commandments which are the most obviously necessary to maintain society would be the first to be revised. Neither Shabbos nor *kashrus*, but rather, murder, stealing, and adultery would perhaps be the first laws to be altered. How do the Sages know that these fundamental laws would be the most vulnerable?

Chazal[17] tell us that before the Torah was given to the Jewish People, it was offered to all the other nations of the world. Upon receiving the offer, each nation wanted to know exactly what was in this Torah. When they heard the answer, however, when they were given an example of what they might expect, they refused to accept it. Actually the very act of asking what was written in the Torah was, in itself, a rejection of God's offer. For when these nations questioned the contents of the Torah, they were already stating that they would accept it only if it suited them. They had no love for God, no desire to fulfill His Will. Theirs was only a self-centered, self-serving mentality. At any rate, the Torah was compatible with them, for it diametrically opposed their lifestyle.

Still, we are prompted to ask: which commandments did God reveal to them? What scared them off? He did not

---

17. *Sifri* on Deuteronomy 33:2.

reveal the laws of Shabbos or *kashrus*. Rather, He forbade murder, stealing and adultery. These nations rejected commandments that are fundamental and essential to humanity. It is upon these commandments that man's attention would be focused if he were able to amend the Torah. Since these commandments are the basis of society and touch man's life in many sensitive and crucial ways, they are the hardest to deal with as absolutes.

Yet aren't these very laws found in all civilized countries? What nation did not or does not outlaw murder, theft, and adultery? Why did the nations of the world reject God's offer if these laws are part of their own societies in any case?

God-Given Versus Man-Made

The answer lies in the fact that there is a world of difference between a God-given law and a law that man accepts upon himself. A God-given law is absolute; man does not have the right or the authority to interpret it according to his convenience. In contrast, a man-made law serves the needs of society. Individuals in that society are willing to refrain from certain behavior in order to receive the protection that the law offers. For example, although an individual may be tempted to steal, he is willing to control his temptations in exchange for the security of knowing that others cannot steal from him. Man-made laws give men the freedom to decide when any given statute does and doesn't apply. These laws also imply a potentially unlimited freedom: if one becomes so strong and powerful that he no longer fears others, he can cast off the burden of any restriction. Whether or not man will ever achieve this feeling of security, the mere awareness of such freedom serves his self-interest.

An absolute Law, however, cannot be molded to serve one's needs. Man can't claim that, for example, this Law doesn't apply to Jews or blacks. Since man did not create the Law, he is not in control. It applies in all situations, in all societies, and at all times. This absoluteness of the Torah, when offered to the nations, precipitated their rejection. They understood that the Torah demanded subordinating themselves to their Creator, and, although they knew that life guided by God's Torah offered them the best possible way of life, these nations could not give up the freedom and convenience of relative ethics.

A Torah that is changeable would provide relative rather than absolute ethics. With relative ethics, man retains the right to make his own judgments. For example, one day the killing of an unborn infant is deemed the most horrible thing a physician could do. His colleagues would look upon him with disapproval and repulsion. He would be ostracized by society. Even if the abortion were necessary for the health of the mother, it would be looked upon with disdain. However, within one year, this same operation can become as casual as drinking a glass of water.

Such shifts in attitude can occur amazingly quickly in a society based on relative ethics, or on a Torah that could be altered. This Torah would have neither permanence nor meaning. In fact, it would not be a Torah in the first place. It would be a mere ritual or a game, but not a way of life. On the other hand, absolute ethics are by definition unchangeable.

A Covenant with the Nations

There is another question that can be asked about the offering of the Torah to the nations of the world and their refusal. The commandments they were given as examples of the Torah, the laws pertaining to murder, stealing, and adultery, are part of the seven Noachide laws. If these nations were already obligated to keep these mitzvos, why should they now reject them?

The nations were offered the opportunity to accept a Torah that would involve a *bris*, a covenant, in order to establish a stronger relationship with the Almighty. A covenant by definition entails the opportunity to either accept or reject it. The nations rejected it. If they could have, they would have rejected the seven Noachide laws as well. However, since these laws are not part of any covenant, there was never any possibility of rejecting them. The Almighty demands that these laws be kept by all humanity, and because He is the Creator and we are His creations, we have no choice but to accept them. Through the fulfillment of these seven laws, *all* mankind can come close to God and earn a share in the World to Come.

However, even these laws are only known to humanity as the Will of God because they were part of the revelation at Sinai, as will soon be discussed. The ramification of this reality is clearly stated by the Rambam:[18] "Everyone [every gentile] who accepts the seven mitzvos and is careful to fulfill them is counted among the Righteous Gentiles of the world. He also has a portion in the World to Come. [But] this is so [only] when he accepts them and fulfills them because God commanded them in His Torah and made it known to us through Moshe Rabbeinu that the children of Noah were previously commanded to do them."

In other words, if gentiles observe these seven mitzvos only because they appreciate their value, understanding how necessary they are, these individuals have no share in the World to Come. They earn this ultimate good only if they fulfill their mitzvos as laws given by the Almighty through Moshe Rabbeinu. Consequently, when they rejected the Torah they also opted out of these laws.

---

18. Rambam, *Mishneh Torah*, Laws of Kings 9:1.

The Eighth Principle

The Divinity of the Torah

We believe that the entire Torah in our posses-
sion today was given [to us] by the Almighty
through Moshe Rabbeinu, by means of the me-
dium we metaphorically call "speech". No one
knows the real nature of this communication
except Moshe, to whom it was transmitted. He
was like a scribe receiving dictation. He wrote
the history, the stories, and the commandments.
Therefore he is called " [the] inscriber".

There is no difference between (Genesis 10:6)
"And the sons of Ham were Cush, Mizraim, Phut,
and Canaan," (Genesis 36:39) "And his wife's
name was Mehetabele, the daughter of Matred,
the daughter of Meizahab," (Genesis 36:12) "And
Timna was concubine to..." and (Deuteronomy
5:6) "I am God, your Lord, who brought you
out of the land of Egypt" and (Deuteronomy
6:4) "Hear O Israel, God is our Lord, God is
One." For it is all from God; it is all God's
perfect Torah, pure, holy and true.

He who says that these verses and stories were
invented by Moshe is considered by our Sages
and prophets to be more heretical and misleading
than any other heretic. For he believes that the
Torah contains both relevant and irrelevant

verses, and he sees the historical passages as useless, and as Moshe's innovations. [He is included among those who say that] the Torah is not from God. [Even] he who believes that the entire Torah was given by God except for one verse (which Moshe wrote) has (Numbers 15:31) "disgraced the word of God." May God rise above the words of the heretics.

Every word in the Torah has wisdom and wondrous insights for those who understand them; [the Torah's] wisdom is unfathomable. [The Torah is] (Job 11:9) "longer than the earth and wider than the sea." One can only follow in the footsteps of David, God's Messiah, who prayed, "Open my eyes that I may behold the wonders of Your Torah" (Psalms 119:18).

The authoritative explanation of the Torah was communicated by God, and the way we observe the commandments of sukkah, lulav, shofar, tzitzis, tefillin, etc., is exactly as God instructed Moshe. He [Moshe] was the faithful conduit [of the Oral Law].

This is the eighth Principle, as affirmed by the verse (Numbers 16:28) "With this you will know that the Almighty sent me to do all these things, for I have not done them of my own mind."

The Eighth Principle

The Divinity of the Torah

The Inscriber of God's Words

The *Ani Ma'amin* version of this Principle reads: "I believe with complete faith that the entire Torah which is now in our possession is the same as that which was given to Moshe Rabbeinu, may he rest in peace." This rendition of the eighth Principle expresses the belief that the Torah we have now is the same Torah that was given to Moshe Rabbeinu at Sinai. Although the phrasing chosen by the author of *Ani Ma'amin* is reminiscent of the actual text of the Rambam, it does not reflect his main concern in this Principle.

The text of this Principle reads:

"We believe that the entire Torah in our possession today was given [to us] by the Almighty through Moshe Rabbeinu, by means of the medium we metaphorically call "speech". No one knows the real nature of this communication except Moshe, to whom it was transmitted. He was like a scribe receiving dictation. He wrote the history, the stories, and the commandments. Therefore he is called [the] 'inscriber'."

Clearly, the thrust of this Principle is the conviction that every letter of the Written and Oral Law transmitted through Moshe Rabbeinu was of Divine origin. Moshe Rabbeinu merely served as a conduit for communicating it, or as a "scribe", as the Rambam himself describes him.

In contrast, it is difficult to understand *Ani Ma'amin* literally, i.e., that the Torah we now possess is the same Torah given to Moshe Rabbeinu. It is true that as long as the Temple stood and the Torah scroll which Moshe Rabbeinu wrote was kept there, the Jewish People had a standard to which to compare all new Torah scrolls that were written. But we are told[19] that after the destruction of the Temple, when Ezra returned to Israel, he found three Torah scrolls which were either considered valid. Even so, there were minor discrepancies among them, which were maintained or discarded depending on whether they appeared in two of the three scrolls. Although the Torah itself instructs Jews to follow the majority in making a decision,[20] one suspects that after many such occurrences, his decisions are not going to produce *absolutely* accurate reproductions of the original Sinai version. The Talmud, too, says we are no longer experts in the exact spelling of many words. Consequently, the rabbis could not count the exact number of letters in the Torah.[21] Certainly, these were very minor variances—such as spelling a word with a *hei* or an *alef*, or with or without a *vav*— changes which did not seem to affect the meaning significantly.

The Rambam knew very well that these variations ex-

---

19. *Sofrim* 6:4.

20. See Exodus 23:2.

21. *Kiddushin* 30a.

isted when he defined his Principles. The words of *Ani Ma'amin* and the words of the Rambam, "the entire Torah in our possession today," must not be taken literally, implying that all the letters of the present Torah are the exact letters given to Moshe Rabbeinu. Rather, it should be understood in a general sense that the Torah we learn and live by is for all intents and purposes the same Torah that was given to Moshe Rabbeinu. The real emphasis of this Principle is that this Torah, which includes both the Written and Oral Law, is word for word, *letter for letter from the Almighty*, and absolutely none of it was edited by Moshe in any way whatsoever. There is not one phrase, not one letter that Moshe added to clarify or explain what was transmitted to him. He had no input of any kind but functioned only as the mouthpiece of the Almighty.

Moshe's Free Will

In order for God to guarantee that Moshe Rabbeinu was a true prophet, as He did at Sinai, and that every word of the Torah is the word of the Almighty, it was necessary to deny Moshe free will in regard to his communicating the Torah. It is self-evident that a promise from the Almighty which defines an individual's actions is incompatible with that individual's free will regarding those actions. Once the Almighty promises that an individual will do something according to His Will, the person has no more choice in the matter. Once God testified to the validity and accuracy of the prophecy of Moshe Rabbeinu, Moshe could no longer edit, add or subtract anything from the words of the Torah, even if he would have wanted to. Perhaps this restriction of free will was the natural consequence of relating to the Almighty "face to face", or perhaps it was a specific intervention, a miracle, in order to assure the giving of the Torah. It is clear, however, that once God promised that Moshe Rabbeinu was a true prophet, he automatically lost his free will in the entire process of communicating the Torah.

The Oral Law

The requisite for this Principle is clear. As mentioned, since only a Torah that is absolute and not open to change can bind man, providing the opportunity for worshipping the Almighty, any ambiguity in the laws of the Torah would render it non-absolute and therefore non-binding. Consequently, the Oral Law was given simultaneously to Moshe Rabbeinu at Sinai, complementing the Written Law. Both together constitute Torah. Without the Oral Law, the Written Law remains ambiguous and cannot bind man to the service of God. That's why the various splinter groups throughout history that have attempted to keep the Written Law without the Oral Law have all but disappeared.

Thus, regarding the Oral Law as well, if Moshe Rabbeinu could have edited or changed a word, there would no longer be a Torah. For anything an individual would not like, anything of inconvenience, *that* would be the very word or idea he would claim that Moshe had changed. As long as the possibility existed of one sentence, one letter being not from God but from man, one could pick and choose whatever he liked.

As discussed, if the Torah is subject to choice, it has no meaning. This is the basic flaw of any segment of Jewry that feels it can choose which laws are relevant and which are not. In essence, these Jews are transforming a body of absolute law and ethics into one of relative law and ethics. As they shift and twist to conform to the passing fantasies and outlooks of society, their tailor-made "Torah" becomes more and more attenuated.

It is in exactly this way that the Catholic Church has lost

its strength. There was a time when Catholics thought the Church professed absolute truth and was not subject to change. Now that Vatican II has allowed various shifts and innovations, however, relatively few people still take the Church seriously. Why should they if tomorrow a new pope will change today's "absolute" law? Why go through the inconvenience of obeying a law only to discover it was all for nothing? As a result, the Church has very little authority left; it has become a culture which will naturally become weaker and weaker with every generation.

The identical phenomena would have occurred with Torah if there ever existed the possibility that one law or another was not from God. In contrast, this Principle states clearly that every word is the Almighty's. The Torah is absolute. There can be no choosing of what to follow and what to reject. There can be no changes without destroying the very fiber of Torah, and without creating a situation where man will no longer be serving God.

The Ninth Principle

The Uniqueness of the Torah

This Torah that Moshe transcribed from the Almighty is unique and there will never be another. One must neither add to it nor subtract from it, be it the Written Law or the Oral Law. As is stated (Deuteronomy 13:1), "Neither add to it nor subtract from it." We have already elaborated upon this Principle in the introduction to this work.

The Ninth Principle

The Uniqueness of the Torah

Never Again Another Sinai

The previous Principle included the tenet that the Torah cannot be changed through prophecy. A prophet has no right to innovate, add, or detract any word or idea from either the Written Law or the Oral Law. Still, one asks: what if God Himself would bring the Jewish Nation back to Sinai or to the Temple—the equivalent of Sinai—and He Himself, in front of the entire Nation, would amend the Torah? This possibility was not discussed in the previous Principle but it is addressed by the ninth Principle. Here it is stated that the Almighty Himself will never give another Torah, nor will He add or detract from the Torah we now possess.

Why is this Principle necessary? One can well understand the need for and significance of stating that man cannot amend the Torah. Man, in all his subjectivity, is influenced by the temptations of his heart, societal changes, and peer pressure. If a prophet were empowered to change the Torah, the Jewish People would have a surplus of "prophets" claiming to have received prophecies that would make their lives easier and more convenient. Fortunately, prophets are not so empowered, saving the Jews from this onslaught. However, if the possibility of changing the Torah does exist for God Himself, what threat does this possibility pose to the reality of Torah and the potential of man in serving the Creator?

Remember, in order for a tenet to be included in these Principles, its awareness and acknowledgement must make the difference between the Jew having an absolute Torah or not. Without each Principle, there would be no body of law that would bind him. Thus, each Principle provides his choice: either to submit to the Will of God or not.

Here, the fact that the Rambam tells us that God will never give another Torah is not being questioned. Rather, we are considering why the revelation at Sinai must necessarily be a unique event, never to be repeated. Why must this be part of these Principles?

The Torah is True for Eternity

The difference between a unique revelation and a revelation which could be repeated is the same as the difference between a Torah that is absolute and a Torah that is relative. The idea that God could change the Torah would generate the suspicion, the possibility, that the Torah is only true for a particular time, situation, or place. Therefore, it could not be absolute. In this situation, the Torah would no longer be the "blueprint of Creation"; rather, it would become a temporary means to fulfill the needs of society. Seen in this context, the Torah might not be deemed appropriate for our electronic age. Obviously, the present society differs dramatically from the society that received the Torah thirty-five hundred years ago. And besides, few if any Jews live in a desert nowadays. From this perspective, a Torah that was given for an agricultural age—or even an industrial age—might be judged totally inadequate and inapplicable to our electronic age. For example, in an agricultural age, in which people perform backbreaking labor, one can appreciate the need for a Shabbos; but in an electronic age, when all that's necessary is the pressing of a few buttons in order to perform a task, doesn't the idea of Shabbos become obsolete?

If, however, we know that there will never be another revelation, if God promises that He will never change a word of the Torah, then every word in the Torah attests to its eternal validity. One can appreciate that Torah mirrors the truth of God Himself, and is therefore the basis of existence. Reflecting on this, it becomes obvious that Torah cannot be affected by any situational change. Lifestyle and environment can never influence the validity or applicability of the Torah, for it is impossible to talk of relevance or irrelevance when you are discussing that which is absolute.

Even the possibility that there *could* be another revelation, although there has not yet been one, would disturb the Jew. The possibility would lead him to reason that there hasn't been another revelation yet only because the Jewish Nation has not been worthy. He would then be very tempted to rationalize and suggest to himself that if the Nation had been worthy, certainly God would have revealed Himself and adapted the Torah to its present lifestyle. This rationalization would be the beginning of the end, for who would wait for the Jewish Nation to become worthy of revelation? Torah would cease to exist because everything in it that is inconvenient to one's lifestyle would begin to apear irrelevant.

With the understanding that Torah is absolute, it is obvious that there is no time when it becomes inappropriate. As a matter of fact, instead we discover that in the entire history of mankind, Shabbos was never more relevant and needed than it is today. There has never been a time like the present, when Shabbos is so necessary in order for us to retain our Judaism as well as to transcend the materialism and hedonism of the modern "me" society. As man's technological accomplishments reach a level of sophistication beyond his greatest expectations, the need to appreciate that he himself is a creation, beholden to his Creator, becomes even greater. Shabbos is the key to spirituality and to the realization that wealth and indulgence are not the totality of human existence. Yet all of these insights appear only after we accept the premise of the Torah being absolute. The nature of man's personality dictates that if there were any potential for change, man would suddenly awaken to "discover" the irrelevance of Shabbos.

In summation, God Himself guarantees that there will be no changes in the Torah. It is absolute, unchangeable truth, reflecting the very nature of Creation, totally relevant in all situations for all time.

Absolute Laws in a Changing World

Understanding the absolute, unchangeable nature of Torah grants us insight into the necessity and essence of the Oral Law.[22] It is the Oral Law which provides the means for the absolute laws and values given at Sinai to be applied to new situations.

How can an absolute Torah address the circumstantial needs of the moment? How does an unchangeable, written

---

22. The Oral Law includes all those laws that were given orally to Moshe Rabbeinu at Sinai. It does not include the laws that are derived from the thirteen hermeneutical principles. Although these principles came from Sinai, their application involves human minds and is therefore subject to change.

Torah relate to a changeable world? For example, the laws pertaining to saying a blessing before we eat are not found in the Torah. Their omission attests to the possibility that a Jew could be so aware that everything he has comes from the Almighty that for him blessings would be an unnecessary reminder. They would not be necessary because he would never make the mistake of considering his good fortune to be the consequence of his own hard work. Therefore, since the possibility of such a consciousness exists, at least theoretically, the law of blessing God as the Source of our sustenance before one eats is not absolute and is therefore not found in the Torah.

However, when a significant number of Jews could no longer depend upon themselves to remember that the food they were about to eat was a gift from the Almighty, the Sages legislated the various laws of blessings. They observed the decline in man's awareness of God as the One who sustains humanity, and they deemed it crucial to have these reminders. While the responsibility and the means of legislating such laws are found in the Torah, and are absolute, the particular laws legislated by the Sages are not.

Part III
Reward and Punishment

The Tenth and Eleventh Principles

God's Omniscience

The Almighty knows the actions of people and does not ignore them. [It is] not like those who say (Ezekiel 8:12), "God has abandoned the land," but rather like [the Scriptures that attest to His scrutiny], as it says (Genesis 6:5), "The Almighty saw that there was great evil perpetrated by man in the land..." and (Genesis 18:20) "The Almighty said, 'The cry of Sodom and Gemorrah is great....'" All this attests to this Principle.

Reward and Punishment

The Almighty rewards him who fulfills the commandments of the Torah and punishes him who transgresses its prohibitions. The greatest reward is [experiencing] the World to Come and the greatest punishment is to be cut off [from this experience]. We have already discussed this [issue] sufficiently. Scripture attests to this Principle, as it says (Exodus 32:32-33), " 'Now, if [only] You will bear their iniquity [concerning the Golden Calf], but if not, erase my name from Your Book.' And the

Almighty responded to Moshe: 'He who sins against Me will be erased from My Book.' " This [statement] affirms that [the Almighty] knows who serves [Him] and who transgresses, and rewards and punishes accordingly.

The Tenth and Eleventh Principles

God's Omniscience
God Reacts to Our Actions

God Knows, Cares, and Rewards

The tenth and eleventh Principles will be discussed together since they are closely related to each other. The tenth Principle states that God is aware of everything about a man, including his thoughts, his speech, and his actions. The eleventh Principle states that God reacts to man's thoughts, speech, and actions through reward and punishment. It is these Principles that assimilated Jews reject in denying the existence of a personal God.

The tenth and eleventh Principles depict God as a judge examining the evidence placed in front of Him, considering the situation and its background, and finally making a decision and issuing a verdict. The significance of these two principles and their depiction of Divine Judgment must be examined. After all, it really isn't necessary for God to be aware of man's actions in order for there to be reward and punishment. Reward and punishment could have been built into creation such that reward would be the automatic consequence of fulfilling a commandment, and punishment the consequence of violating one. This alternative reflects a model world into which justice was programmed as a natural outgrowth of various actions. In this system, there would be no need for man to be cognizant of God's awareness of his actions, since even if the Almighty did not know our actions, reward and punishment would exist as an automatic response to man's behavior. Indeed, some scholars maintain this position.[1] The Rambam, however, by including the tenth Principle, asserts that man must know that God is aware of his actions in order to exist with a sense of meaning. Why is this awareness necessary? What is the tenth Principle telling us?

Prudence or Love

There is a difference between an action motivated by an awareness of the consequences which automatically follow it, and an action motivated by an awareness of the reaction of the Almighty. It is the difference between acting out of prudence and acting out of love. It is the difference between acting for oneself and acting for another. In a programmed world, where consequences are automatic, the individual has only himself to consider. In a non-programmed world, man considers and relates to God's response.

Giving Life Meaning

In the introduction to this work, it was mentioned that an awareness of reward and punishment is essential for the relationship man has with God. Without God's response to

---

1. See the discussion of reward and punishment in the beginning of *Shnei Luchos HaBris.*

his actions, man could not serve Him, for no relationship can exist on a unilateral basis. The Almighty's awareness of man's actions, and His responding to them with what man views as reward and punishment, is a sign that He cares. It signifies that one's actions make a difference. Considering the alternative, the model world where justice is built automatically into creation, the promise of an impersonal reward and the threat of punishment would not be enough to motivate man to pursue the morally correct action.

This insight is the message that is conveyed through this Principle. It is imperative to know that God responds to man's actions. Because *He* will respond to *me*, I can feel that my behavior makes a difference. This difference gives meaning, purpose, and justification to life. Life has meaning when one has a relationship with the Almighty, and this relationship is predicated upon the reality of His response to our actions. A built-in reward and punishment system indicates indifference, and would destroy any possibility of a relationship between man and God. By including the tenth Principle, that God is aware of our actions, the Rambam is denying the possibility of a mechanical universe and asserting the truth of God's "personal" response to our actions.

It is this personal, caring response from God towards His People which Moshe Rabbeinu described as he prepared the Jewish Nation to receive the Torah:[2] "You have seen what I did to Egypt and how I carried you on the wings of eagles and brought you to Me." At first glance, one would think that in order to motivate and inspire the Nation to accept the Torah, Moshe Rabbeinu is focusing its attention on the might and grandeur of the Almighty, who defeated the strongest nation in the world and enabled the Jews to escape from their iron prison. Yet Rashi understands the statement "You have seen

---

2. Exodus 19:4.

what I did to Egypt" in a much more profound way. He states that Moshe Rabbeinu wanted to call the Nation of Israel's attention to the fact that although Egypt had been steeped in immorality and deserving of punishment long before the exodus, the Almighty, with His unlimited patience, had waited and delayed retribution. The persecution of the Jews, however, brought an end to God's patience, and He let loose His wrath against the Egyptians. Just as a father warns the bullies on the block: "Do what you want—just stay clear of my kid," God's delay served as a warning to Egypt. Therefore, Rashi explains, Moshe Rabbeinu pointed out to his Nation the love and caring that God had demonstrated by causing the exodus at exactly that time in history. Without this awareness of God's love, the Jews would not have trusted Him enough to commit themselves to His Torah.

The Greatest Kindness

God's love and concern are manifest through His judgment of us on Rosh HaShanah. The concept of *Malchus*—the King who sits upon the Throne of Judgment—is the theme of the Yom Tov. God is aware and He cares. He cares so much for His creations that He Himself judges them, weighing and assessing the actions of each one of His children. Rosh HaShanah is the beginning of the Ten Days of Repentance, during which—we are told by the Sages—the Almighty comes close to man. Man is urged to "search for Him while He is to be found,"[3] return to Him while He is so close. People understand the Sages' words to mean that because God is about to judge man, He performs a special act of kindness by making Himself available to him before the final decision. However, these words really mean that the

---

3. Isaiah 55:6; see *Rosh HaShanah* 18a; Rambam, *Mishneh Torah*, Laws of Repentance 2:6.

very process of judgment itself is the greatest act of kindness that the Almighty could bestow upon man. The act of judging, of relating to man, is exactly what creates the closeness to which the Sages are referring.

This kindness explains why Rosh HaShanah comes before Yom Kippur. One would think that the Ten Days of Repentance and Yom Kippur, the Day of Atonement, should have come first, before the Day of Judgment. Shouldn't God judge man after he has repented, after there has been atonement for his sins?

In order to appreciate the answer to this question, one must remember that an entire year has passed since the last period of repentance. Over this year, people become callous to the reality of judgment. They forget how important their actions are, becoming insensitive to the fact that what they do makes a difference because the Almighty cares. Accordingly, the answer to this question is that only the traumatic experience of being judged, of experiencing the awesome relationship of God judging man, rescues man from his apathy and inspires him to return to the Almighty. Once man regains the awareness that God is a King who cares, only then is he prepared to critically examine his life. Until one is aware of the God who judges, the God who cares, he cannot appreciate the God who forgives and grants atonement to His People.

The Twelfth Principle

The Messianic Era

[We] believe and affirm that the Mashiach will come. One should not think he is detained. [Rather,] (Habakkuk 2:3) "If he should tarry, await him."

One is not to assign him a specific time of arrival, nor should one use Scripture to deduce when he is coming. For the Sages have said: "The souls of those who calculate the end will be shattered."

[One must also] believe that [the Mashiach] will surpass all the kings who have ever ruled in terms of his grandeur, his greatness, and his honor. [Man should] exalt, love, and pray for him according to the prophecies prophesied about him by all the prophets from Moshe Rabbeinu to Malachi.

He who doubts or belittles [the Mashiach's arrival] denies [the authority of the Torah, which explicitly promises his arrival] in the story of Bilaam and in Deuteronomy 30.

Included within this Principle is [the idea] that the king of Israel must come from the House of David and the seed of Solomon. Anyone who opposes this dynasty defies the Almighty and the words of His prophets.

The Twelfth Principle
The Messianic Era

A World without Mashiach

Realization of this Principle is not easy because it involves more than awareness and conviction. It demands feelings and thoughts that can only be the products of a very special way of life.

In his *Mishneh Torah*,[4] the Rambam says: "Anyone who does not believe in him [the Mashiach] or does not await his coming not only denies [the truth of his coming, as stated in] the rest of the prophets, he denies Torah and [the prophecy of] Moshe Rabbeinu." What is meant by "awaiting his coming"? Must one think that he is going to come today? What if today is Shabbos or Yom Tov? Concerning this Principle, *Ani Ma'amin* states, "I believe with complete faith in the coming of the Mashiach, and even if he should tarry, I nevertheless will wait every day for his coming." Does this "waiting every day" apply to

---

4. Laws of Kings 11:1.

Shabbos and Yom Tov, as one would assume?

Actually, our tradition tells us that the Mashiach will not come on Shabbos or Yom Tov.[5] Therefore, one need not anticipate his coming at every moment. What is more, in his *Commentary to the Mishnah*,[6] the Rambam says, "Whoever doubts or minimizes his [the Mashiach's] importance denies the Torah that attests to it." Instead of the need to await his coming, which the Rambam discussed in *Mishneh Torah*, here he warns against minimizing the Mashiach's importance. It would seem, then, that "awaiting him" should be understood as attributing to him so much importance that one is aware of missing something, of lacking something every moment of one's life. It is not enough to know and believe in his coming; one must also feel and understand what it means not to have him in our world.

A world without the Mashiach is a world of exile, where Jews find themselves dispersed amongst many nations. It is a world where even in the Land of Israel, Jews are subjected to the whims and values of other nations. It is a world in which terrible barriers created by spiritual apathy deter man from coming close to the Almighty, and where the opportunities to approach Him and to experience His presence in His Temple are gone. Once one appreciates that the meaning of life is determined by how close one comes to the Creator, the loss of His presence becomes an acute, intolerable pain, a cancer, which eats away at man's spiritual core, which can only be anesthetized by distracting ourselves through all kinds of self-delusionary pleasures. In doing so, mankind has become callous and his senses have become dull to the ultimate pleasure this relationship would offer.

---

5. *Eiruvin* 43b.

6. *Sanhedrin* 10:1

A Jew without Mashiach

There is no greater destructiveness for the Jewish soul than to lose the awareness of the bitterness of exile. When Jews become too comfortable in the diaspora with their nice homes, their cars, and yes, even their yeshivos, they start forgetting what is missing from their lives. They no longer feel the pain of exile. The comfort, leisure and affluence have contributed to the distortion of Torah, resulting in another approach to Judaism, an approach actually found amongst believing Jews who accept the Torah and its mitzvos. Those who adhere to this approach still recognize man's debt to his Creator. They still recognize the need to acknowledge the Almighty as the Source of health, material wellbeing and comfort, and even existence itself.

They are willing to pay this debt to the fullest extent. Since this entails heeding God's commandments, they are willing to fulfill this obligation, just as they give a certain required amount of money to taxes, but no more. There is no concern for reaching beyond the letter of the law in order to enhance or safeguard their relationship with God. In questionable situations, lenient interpretations are always sought. The Torah's commandments are burdens that make the pursuit of a Western, hedonistic way of life difficult.

These people do, however, manage to observe the commandments while living this way of life. Yet, unfortunately, it is impossible to discuss with them the bitterness of *galus*, of exile. They would question: Why should one yearn for the coming of the Messianic era? What is missing now? This approach is wholly inconsistent with the twelfth Principle, that one must await the coming of the Mashiach. How different they are from those whose lives are dedicated to coming closer to the Almighty. These Jews know and feel God's existence to the extent that nothing else has meaning in their lives. They exemplify the true approach. They use the resources of an affluent society only insofar as it contributes to this ultimate pleasure of drawing close to God. They can well understand the words of the Rambam, the feeling of eagerly awaiting the coming of Mashiach and the era he will herald.

No observant Jew will question the coming of the Messianic era as a tenet of Judaism. However, as one of the Thirteen Principles, this idea denotes much more. Here, awareness of the coming of the Mashiach becomes part of the body of information that makes it possible for a member of the Jewish People to relate to the Almighty. Anyone who lacks this awareness, even if only because he was never taught, cannot be considered a practicing Jew.

Why should this tenet be so crucial? The necessity of consciously accepting the first five Principles, which deal with the existence of God, can be understood easily. No matter how good one's intentions are, if he has a misconception concerning the nature of God, he cannot correctly relate to Him or accept His sovereignty. The significance of the next four Principles, dealing with God's communication to man, is also self-evident. One cannot practice Judaism if he is not aware of the Torah being the Will of God. It has likewise been explained that awareness of reward and punishment is also essential in order to relate to the Almighty because it is impossible to serve an indifferent Creator. But why is it imperative to know that history will culminate in the coming of the Mashiach?

The Providence that Shapes History

Man can accept the sovereignty of God only when he is aware of the Almighty's love, concern, and providence. He cannot relate to an indifferent God. Failing to see Divine providence in history translates into failing to see the Almighty reacting to man's actions. How many perceived the Holocaust as the "death of God," demanding, "Where was God's love for His chosen Nation?" This perception was due to their doubting whether there really was Divine providence. If the Jews were indeed chosen, how could this happen to them? And not only the Holocaust! There seems to be no end to anti-Semitism. Can one study history, especially the history of the Jewish People, without becoming depressed? Where is the Almighty's guidance?

Without the certainty of the Messianic era, these questions would remain unanswered. Without Mashiach, the Jew would find it impossible to relate to the Almighty as a loving and caring Father. This Principle foretells of the time when the entire world will become aware of God's love for Israel and understand the Providence that shapes history. Not only do these predictions provide hope for Israel during the gloom and despair of persecution, but they prevent the Jew from perceiving the Almighty's providence as a farce. For thousands of years, the Jew has survived the horrors of a bitter exile, knowing that the fate of his Nation will eventually change and that someday all of mankind will come to know its Creator through his People.

Everyone, a Member of the Klal

Another dimension of this Principle is also closely related to man's perception of Divine providence. One thing that can be said with certainty is that the knowledge of Mashiach is not so crucial because of how the Messianic era will affect all Jews individually. Of the millions of Jews who have lived from Sinai until now, relatively few of them will be touched personally by the coming of Mashiach. For if the Mashiach arrives today, only those alive today will be affected.

Therefore, the Jew can only relate to the Messianic era in terms of the Nation of Israel. It is the Nation of Israel that is affected by Mashiach, not the individuals of Israel. Thus, when the Rambam states that the coming of the Mashiach is one of the Thirteen Principles, he is saying that each person's awareness of his role as a member of *Klal Yisrael* is essential. A Jew must be aware that he is not only an individual, but a cell in the body of a nation. If one has the impression that he relates to God as an individual in his own merit and that the Torah was given to him as an individual, he cannot serve the Almighty. Only as part of the Nation can Jews relate to the Torah and the Almighty.

The Maharal goes to great lengths to show that although Abraham was worthy of receiving the Torah, the Torah could only be given to a nation.[7] The Torah is not given to individuals; it must be given to a people. Therefore, this Principle is essential to all Jews, not as individuals but as parts of a nation. The primary justification for the existence of the Jews, then, is as a nation.

This Principle implies that one cannot be a Jew on his own. One can only learn Torah, pray, and perform God's many other commandments as part of the Nation of Israel, a nation which consists of people who together form one unit. The individuals within this nation are like the cells of one organism.

Only with this realization can one appreciate his connection to Torah. For after all, those generations who came after Sinai never said,[8] "We will do and we will understand"; they never accepted the Torah personally. So what obligates

---

7. Maharal, *Tiferes Yisrael*, ch. 17.
8. Exodus 19:8. Even though, according to Kabbalah, the souls of all Jews were present at Sinai, the soul is not the individual. Rather, the individual is body and soul together.

them to fulfill it? What connects them to the experience at Sinai? Since none of them ever entered into a verbal or written covenant of accepting the Torah with the Almighty, as individuals there would seem to be nothing to bind them. They are bound and committed to the Covenant only because they are part of a nation. It was necessary for the entire Nation to be at Sinai in order for the commitment to be a national commitment, and the unity of the people was critical, as it is written: " 'Israel camped at the foot of the mountain [preparing to receive the Torah]'—like one man with one heart."[9] This is the nation that said at Mount Sinai, "We will do and we will understand."

Today, the Jewish People is still "one man". It exists today as a nation just as it did thousands of years ago. Individuals die, like the cells of an organism, but the organism survives with new cells. Although the cells of the organism are different from the cells it was born with, it is still the same organism. God promised that the Nation will never die. The Nation is eternal, and individuals are Jews only because they are part of this eternal Nation. Their serving and relating to God is dependent upon their being part of this Nation. This Principle above all demands that Jews not isolate themselves from their People. They must share in the pain and joy of their fellow Jews, no matter where they are.

Now that this Principle has been redefined in terms of the importance of the Nation, the prospect of eagerly awaiting the Mashiach takes on a new dimension. Waiting for him means knowing that he will bring the world to the recognition of the Almighty and at last fulfill the national mission of Israel. In awaiting him, Jews must always keep in mind their mission as part of the Jewish Nation.

---

9. Rashi on Exodus 19:2, noting that the Hebrew verb used in the verse is singular in order to stress the unity of the people.

The Purpose of Existence

The essence of this Principle is that Jews be aware of the purpose of their nation and their existence. In turn, the more one yearns for the Messianic era, the more he commits himself to the fulfillment of this purpose. Without the recognition of this ultimate revelation of God, the Jew would perceive his worship as one-sided and futile. Torah, the covenantal relationship between the Jew and the Almighty, can only be adhered to when man is aware of the reciprocity of that relationship, and the Mashiach is that reciprocity. The Messianic era is the Almighty's response to the efforts of the Jewish People. Without the awareness of this response, the Jew would be forced to find other avenues of meaning and purpose. That is why the awareness and acceptance of Mashiach is a Principle.

The Thirteenth Principle

The Resurrection of the Dead

The resurrection of the dead is a basic principle of the Torah of Moshe. Anyone who does not believe in it has no connection with the Jewish Nation. But [resurrection] is only for the righteous, as it states in Bereishis Rabbah: "Rain is for both the righteous and the wicked but resurrection is for the righteous alone." For how can the wicked be brought back to life when even during their lives they are considered dead? But the righteous, even when they die, are considered alive.

The Thirteenth Principle

The Resurrection of the Dead

Why Resurrection?

It would be easy to understand if this final Principle, the last of the four Principles dealing with reward and punishment, had been belief in the World to Come. After all, how can one believe in absolute justice without such a conviction? Where is there true reward and punishment in a world where so many innocent and righteous suffer while so many evil people seem to enjoy the good life? If this world is all there is, how can a system of reward and punishment be perceived to exist? If, however, this world is not an end in itself, then reward and punishment may be understood to be found in an afterlife. There, the consequences of one's actions in this world will be realized.

So again, why doesn't this Principle posit the existence of the World to Come? Why did the Rambam choose the idea of the resurrection of the dead instead?

Actually, resurrection and the World to Come are part

of the same concept, for resurrection is the beginning of the World to Come. Before the resurrection, no one partakes of the World to Come. Our tradition tells us that the souls of the dead await resurrection in Gan Eden. There is also a soul-cleansing place, Gehinnom, which, in a sense, is also a reward from God. Once one reaches Gehinnom, he is assured of being prepared for the World to Come. Obviously, it is preferable to avoid this reward if at all possible. Nonetheless, souls that have gone through Gehinnom do join with those that went straight to Gan Eden, and there they all await the "great and awesome Day of Judgment" which prophets discuss.[10] This Day of Judgment is the day of the resurrection of the dead, when all will be judged as to their position in the World to Come. Until resurrection, no human being enters the World to Come.

Still, why does the Rambam describe this Principle in terms of resurrection rather than the World to Come?

The Immortal Body

Man is not a soul bound in a transient body. If that were the case, resurrection would have little significance other than representing the soul's return to its bodily prison. Man is a soul and a body together. As such, he needs to relate to a future that somehow involves both his soul and his body. Resurrection is the rejoining of the body to the soul in such a way that it can achieve this future. If the World to Come involved only the soul, would man be willing to give his body's entire life for a future nothingness? The soul has always been understood to be immortal; it never dies. We comprehend the immortality of the human being, however, through the resurrection of the body. Resurrection signifies that man in his totality, body and soul, is immortal.

---

10. Malachi 3:23.

The relationship of body and soul is like that of a blind man and a lame man.[11] The lame man sees delicious fruit in a nearby orchard but can't reach it. The blind man can reach it but doesn't see it. Thus, the lame man instructs the blind man to carry him across the field, with the lame man directing him to the fruit. The blind man happily agrees and anxiously they advance into the orchard and take the fruit.

Soon afterward, the outraged orchard owner appears and begins to question them. The blind man says, "I couldn't have taken the fruit—I can't see." The lame man says, "I couldn't have taken the fruit—I can't walk." The owner thinks a moment and then forces the lame man to hop onto the shoulders of the blind man. Only then, when they are together, has the owner found his culprit, so he beats them both.

Just as there could be no punishment for the lame man alone, there can be no reward or punishment for the soul. Alone, it cannot sin. A soul only sins in its body. Reward and punishment can only apply to the entity that is the person, the body and soul together. Only thus can justice be meted out. The soul cannot enter the World to Come without the body. Is it possible that once the entity of body and soul achieves a place in the World to Come, the body is discarded? A soul is not an image of God. A body is not an image of God. The soul doesn't have free will and the body doesn't have free will. Only the two together have free will, only the two together are the image of God. The union of body and soul is what makes us greater than the angels. As Moshe Rabbeinu pointed out to the angels, it is because of this unique body-soul union that the Jewish Nation received the Torah.[12] This union manifests itself in the thirteenth

---

11. *Sanhedrin* 91b.
12. *Shabbos* 88b-89a.

Principle, according to which the body, in a sense, attains immortality along with the soul.

The Resurrection of the Physical

The Rambam says there will be no eating, drinking or sleeping in the World to Come.[13] This statement was the focal point of a dispute between the Rambam and the Ramban, and has been deeply misunderstood. In the World to Come, the body will not be resurrected and then die. The Rambam says that after resurrection, the body will cease to be a body as we know it.[14] This cessation implies that the body will instead become so holy that it will become spiritual, transcending the physical limitations imposed upon it in this earthly world. Nevertheless, it will retain its sense of self-existence, its sense of being. The Ramban disagrees with the Rambam's assertion that the resurrected body will eventually cease to exist in a physical sense. He believes that the body will always have its physical limitations, which are necessary for it to be aware of itself.

In this state of spirituality, in knowing the Creator, man will reach a level of ecstasy beyond our mortal grasp. As the prophet[15] describes it, "no eye has ever seen [it]." The World to Come is inconceivable; the prophet himself cannot describe it. It is beyond the conception of a created human being to comprehend what it means to be connected to the Source of all existence.

The foolishness is evident when people say: "What could be more boring than Heaven!" Of course, they are imagining Heaven in terms of the sensual pleasures of this world. The

---

13. Rambam, *Mishneh Torah*, Laws of Repentance 8:2.
14. Ibid.
15. Isaiah 64:3; see *Berachos* 34b.

reason that sensual pleasures in excess do not satisfy, and may even become disgusting, is because they aren't true pleasures in ultimate terms. For the most part, they serve as an escape from the pain and effort of striving for real pleasure.

The feeling of total "being", on the other hand, the sense of accomplishment, of reaching one's ultimate goals, is true pleasure which can be grasped even in this world. The joy of a child whose parents admire the picture he has drawn, the thrill of solving a difficult problem, or the glee on the face of a youngster who has brought home a perfect report card—all are true but still only partial experiences of the ultimate pleasure.

This ultimate experience of being connected with actual, absolute Existence requires the whole being, the body as well as the soul. Without resurrection, without man's knowing that he, as he now perceives himself, will experience this pleasure, the idea of the World to Come is irrelevant. People are not impressed with their soul existing in the World to Come. They can't relate to such an existence because they feel that their soul alone is just not their whole self.

The Principle of resurrection implies that the body is not merely an object but a subject. The body is part of the person himself. Hence the obligations to bury and honor a dead body. Conversely, Judaism forbids cremation and the use of corpses for theoretical research, since both treat the human body as an object.

Asceticism—A Jewish Approach

Another insight one can glean from this Principle, which comes as a surprise to some since it differs from many other religions, is that the Torah does not castigate the body or its drives. In order to come close to the Almighty, one does not have to humiliate the body or suppress its drives. Monasticism is not the Jewish path to saintliness. Christianity sees the soul as being trapped in the body; therefore, anything that weakens the body supposedly allows the soul to emerge. In contrast, this Principle declares that such an approach is perverted. For if the body were a villain, then why would God create a resurrection to drag it back into being? In Judaism, a person is not just a soul but a body and soul together.

When a person affirms all these Principles, and clarifies his faith in them, he becomes part of the Jewish People. It is a mitzvah to love him, have mercy on him, and show him all the love and brotherhood that God has instructed us to show our fellow Jews. Even if he has transgressed out of desire and the overpowering influence of his base nature, he will be punished accordingly but he will have a share in the World to Come. He is considered a transgressor of Israel. But one who denies any of these Principles has excluded himself from the Jewish People and denied the essence [of Judaism]. He is called a heretic, an apikorus, and "one who has cut off the seedlings". It is a mitzvah to hate such a person, as it says (Tehillim 139:21), "Those who hate You, God, I shall hate."

Conclusion

To Approach the Creator

The Thirteen Principles are the tenets that, in the eyes of the Rambam, define the awareness and commitment necessary to relate to God and His Torah as a member of the Jewish People. These Principles serve as the basis of one's awareness and perspective as he approaches a mitzvah. A lack of awareness and commitment to any of these Principles estranges one from the Jewish community and constricts his ability to fulfill his People's covenant with the Almighty. As discussed, the twelfth Principle implies that the Jew relates to God and to Torah as a member of a nation rather than as an individual. The ramification of this concept, the threat of being alienated from the Jewish community, necessarily affects one's relationship with the Almighty and with Torah, and is the basis of these Principles. Therefore, a lack of awareness of even one of these Principles inevitably impedes the fulfillment of any mitzvah and undermines one's relationship with his fellow Jews, the Torah, and the Almighty. Although some authorities would partially disagree with this

last statement, no one would question the relevance of en-
hancing one's understanding and awareness of these Principles, nor would anyone deny that this endeavor serves as
an invaluable tool in coming closer to the Creator.